Little Giant® Book
of
AFTER
SCHOOL
FUN

Sheila Anne Barry, Paul Sloane
Tom Bullimore, Mark Danna & Trip Payne

*

Illustrated by Jeff Sinclair, Myron Miller,
Ian Anderson & Doug Anderson

Sterling Publishing Co., Inc
New York

10 9 8 7 6 5 4 3 2 1

Published by Sterling Publishing Company, Inc.
387 Park Avenue South, New York, N.Y. 10016
© 2000 by Sterling Publishing Company, Inc.
The games and puzzles in this book have been excerpted from the
following publications: *Super-Colossal Book of Puzzles, Tricks and Games*
© 1978 by Sterling Publishing Company, Inc.; *Baker Street Puzzles* ©
1992 by Tom Bullimore/Knight Features; *Word Search Puzzles for Kids* ©
1999 by Mark Danna; *Crosswords for Kids* © 1999 by Trip Payne; *Lateral
Thinking Puzzlers* © 1991 by Paul Sloane
Distributed in Canada by Sterling Publishing
c/o Canadian Manda Group, One Atlantic Avenue, Suite 105 Toronto,
Ontario, Canada M6K 3E7
Distributed in Great Britain and Europe by Chris Lloyd
463 Ashley Road, Parkstone, Poole, Dorset, BH14 0AX, England
Distributed in Australia by Capricorn Link (Australia) Pty Ltd.
P.O. Box 6651, Baulkham Hills, Business Centre,
NSW 2153, Australia

Sterling ISBN 0-8069-7149-5

Contents

Before You Begin _____ 5

Optical Illusions _____ 7

Mind Reading _____ 29

Crosswords _____ 57

Card Tricks _____ 76

Card Games for One _____ 99

Card Games for Two or More _____ 131

Lateral Thinking Mysteries _____ 161

Word Search Puzzles _____ 195

Sherlock Holmes Mysteries _____ 214

Can You Do It? _____ **241**

Paper & Pencil Games _____ **257**

Games of Skill or Strength _____ **271**

More Great Games _____ **289**

Answers _____ **319**

Index & Guide _____ **345**

Before You Begin

So—school's out—and you don't know what to do with yourself? If you've got this book, you have a lot of choices. And you don't need special equipment for any of them, just ordinary things you've got around the house.

You could start by leafing through the pages of optical illusions—there are 20 of them—find out what makes them work, and maybe invent some of your own.

Or you could learn to do some mind-reading tricks. They look mysterious, but they're easy to do with the instructions here.

You could work some crossword puzzles—all with definitions you stand a good chance of guessing (no words nobody ever heard of just meant to stump you). There are word search puzzles, too, with great themes, like "The Simpsons," "Monopoly," or "Oh, Horrors!"

If you've got a deck of cards, you can master some

terrific card tricks, play a dozen of the best solitaire games, and—if a friend comes over—select from a bunch of the best card games for two or more.

Then there are the mysteries! Start with lateral thinking mysteries—hints are included, if you want them—which you can solve alone or in a group. Go on to Sherlock Holmes mysteries and pit your wits against Professor Moriarty or the great sleuth himself.

If you have paper and pencil (and who doesn't), try your hand at the classic games for one or two or more. Or, if you'd like a little more activity, glance at the challenges in "Can You Do It?," which can give you hours of fun, or the games of skill and strength.

Also included are some of the greatest games of all time, from "20 Questions" to" Mancala," and ways to "psychoanalyze" your friends or tell their fortunes —with tea leaves, dominoes, or dice.

If you can't figure out what to do first, check out the index and guide, starting on page 345. You can make your choices by type—mystery, game, optical illusion, mind reading, puzzle, trick, challenge—or by number of players. Whatever you decide to do—have fun! That's what this book is all about!

—The Authors

CHANGING IMAGES

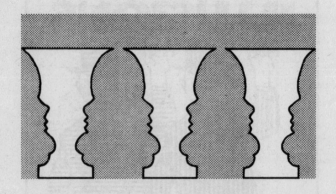

Faces—or vases?

Answer on page 320

THREE MOVIE BUFFS

Which of these moviegoers is the tallest?

Answer on page 320

SICK CIRCLE

What is the matter with this circle?

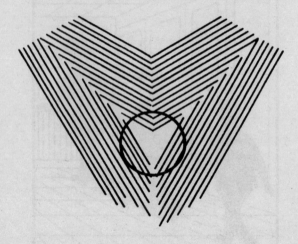

Answer on page 320

BULGING SQUARE

Are the sides of this square bulging out?

Answer on page 320

THE FENCE

Concentrate very hard on a point in the white field of intersecting lines for about 30 seconds. Then shift your attention quickly to one of the black squares. What do you see between the black squares?

Answer on pages 320–321

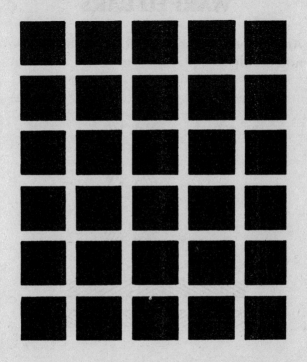

WARPED BARS

Are the white bars straight or do they bulge and bend?

Answer on page 321

WHAT'S ON WHITE?

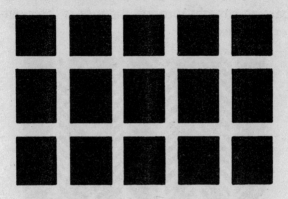

What shows up on the intersecting white lines, even though they are all white?

Answer on page 321

NIGHTMARE FOREST

Are the vertical lines straight? Do the cross-bars go straight through them or is their pattern uneven?

Answer on page 321

MAD HAT

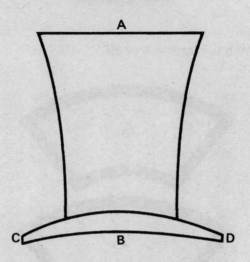

A

C   B   D

How does the height of this top hat (A–B) compare with the width of its brim (C–D)?

Answer on page 322

CUT-OUTS

Which is larger—A or B?

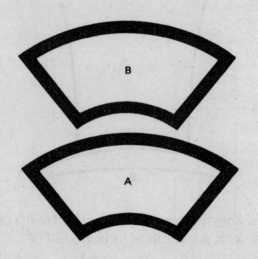

Answer on page 322

UNSURE LINES

1. Is the diagonal line straight?
2. Which line is the continuation of A? B or C?

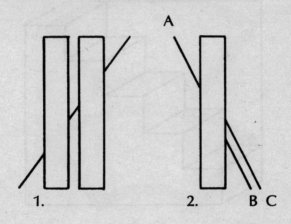

1.

2.

A

B C

Answer on page 322

THE STAIRCASE

A normal staircase? Try walking on it upside down!

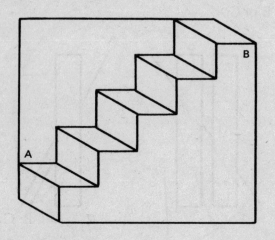

Answer on page 322

LOOKING AROUND

Are you looking inside a tube? Or at the top of a beach ball?

Answer on page 322

FOUR DETECTIVES

Which detective has the largest mouth?

Answer on page 323

HIDDEN SHAPES

In the next three puzzles, each shape is hidden once (same size) in its corresponding diagram. For example, shape #1 is hidden in drawing #1. Can you find the shapes with your naked eye?

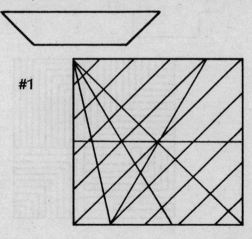

#1

Answer on page 323

See the instructions for "Hidden Shapes" on page 23.

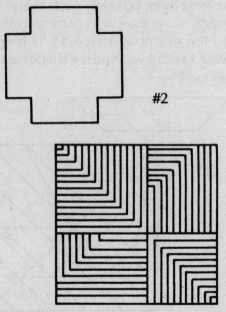

#2

Answer on page 323

THE SPOKE-WHEEL PHENOMENON

How many tiles do you need to cover the floor? Do you get it?

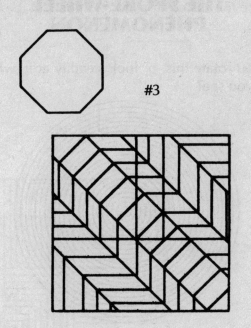

#3

Answer on page 323

THE SPOKE-WHEEL
PHENOMENON

If you rotate this, or look steadily at it, what do you see?

Answer on page 323

BIG WHEELS

Holding the page flat in front of you, move the book in a circle clockwise. What happens to the outside circles? What happens to the cogwheel in the middle?

Answer on page 323

COUNT THE CUBES

Are there 7 cubes here? Or 8?

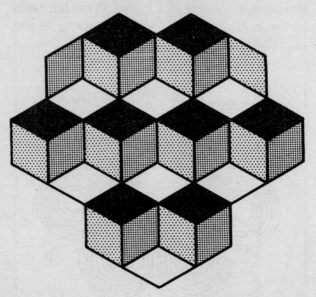

Answer on page 323

MIND
READING

THE MYSTERIOUS TEMPLE

EQUIPMENT: None

THE EFFECT: You leave the room while the group thinks of a number from 1 to 5. When you return, you go around the group, pressing your hands to the temples of each of the players. Feeling their heads, you get "thought waves" from them and—by the time one round is completed—you announce the number the group had in mind!

HOW IT IS DONE: You will always guess the right number, because you're not guessing. You have a spy or partner working for you. The spy clenches and unclenches teeth while you press his or her temples. If the number is 3, the spy clenches teeth three times. That way you get the correct "thought wave."

    Feel your own temples as you clench your

teeth and you will see that this movement causes a ripple which you can feel easily.

Anyone who doesn't know the trick will think you are performing miracles!

SEEING THROUGH A
SEALED ENVELOPE

EQUIPMENT: 4 cards, each about 3 x 4 inches (7.5
    x 10 cm) in size. An envelope just large
    enough to hold a card comfortably.

PREPARATION: Draw a different symbol on each
    card: a circle, a square, a triangle, an X.

THE EFFECT: Show the cards to the spectators. Call their attention to the symbols on the cards.

While you turn away, someone puts one of the cards into the envelope, seals it, and hides the other cards. You take the envelope, hold it to your head, concentrate, and name the symbol on the card. When the envelope is opened, this proves to be correct.

HOW IT IS DONE: Although the cards seem to be identical in size, they vary slightly in their dimensions. That is the subtle secret of the trick. One card, which bears the circle, is just the size of the envelope, slipping in easily but snugly.

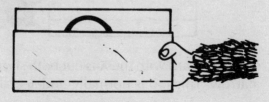

The card with the square on it is cut $1/16$th of an inch (1–2 mm) short. This is too slight a difference to be noticed, even when you handle the cards as a group.

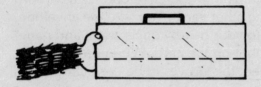

The card with the triangle is cut slightly narrow. The spectators won't notice that either. The difference is about $1/16$th of an inch.

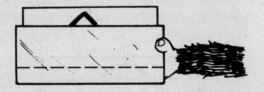

The card with the X is cut both short and narrow. This too is normally undetectable.

After a card is sealed in the envelope, however, you can check the difference swiftly and secretly by holding the opposite edges of the envelope between the thumb and finger and pressing slightly.

It there is no "give" in either direction, the "circle" card is in the envelope. If there is "give" from top to bottom but not sideways, it is the "square" card. If the envelope yields to sideways pressure only, it contains the "triangle" card. If pressure shows slack in both directions, the "X" card is inside.

THE NINE SLIPS

EQUIPMENT: A sheet of paper with smooth edges. A pencil. A hat—or deep bowl.

THE EFFECT: Tear a sheet of paper into nine slips, all the same size. A spectator—say, Linda—writes any name on a slip, folds it, and drops it into a hat or deep bowl.

Now she writes other names on the remaining slips, folds them the same way, and mixes them in the hat.

While Linda concentrates on the original name, you read through the slips one by one and finally announce the name that Linda has in mind!

HOW IT IS DONE: Use a sheet of paper with smooth edges. If necessary, cut any rough edges with a pair of scissors beforehand. Fold the paper into thirds—both ways—so it can be torn into nine equal pieces.

Do this neatly, so the slips look alike, but one of them—the original center of the sheet—will be slightly different. It will have four rough edges, whereas every other slip will have at least one smooth edge.

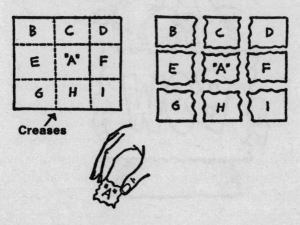

Hand the slip with the four rough edges to Linda first, or put it on top of the others so that she uses it to write the name she has in mind. More names are written on the remaining slips, but you can always pick out the right one by its four rough edges.

I'VE GOT YOUR NUMBER

EQUIPMENT: 7 square cards.
PREPARATION: Write a number on each card, as
    described below.

THE EFFECT: You show the seven square cards
to the group. One person, George, let's say,
notes a number, and you lay the cards facedown in a circle.

You tap the cards in a jumbled way while George spells his number mentally, letter by letter.

Suppose George spells "T-W-E-L-V-E," and on the final letter, says "Stop!" You turn the card up and, by an amazing coincidence, it is George's number—12!

HOW IT IS DONE: Each number is spelled with a different number of letters, so the count works automatically. The numbers on the cards are:

2— T-W-O
5— F-I-V-E
7— S-E-V-E-N
11— E-L-E-V-E-N
16— S-I-X-T-E-E-N
13— T-H-I-R-T-E-E-N
17— S-E-V-E-N-T-E-E-N

When you place the cards in a circle, you arrange them as follows:

Make the first two taps on any cards, but on the third tap, hit the 2, so that if George spells "T-W-O," he will say "Stop!" and you will turn up his card.

For the next tap, jump two cards clockwise, hitting the 5. The next jump is two more, to the 7; then to the 11, and so on around the circle, so that you will automatically turn up the right number on the word "Stop!"

THREE-DIGIT MIRACLE

Take any 3-digit number, 197 for example.

Write it backwards:		791
Subtract the smaller number:		−197
	Total:	594
Now write 594 backwards:		+495
And add it:		1089

What's so miraculous about that? No matter what 3-digit number you use, you'll *always* come up with 1089!

NOTE: If you get the number 99 as the "total" number, look out. Remember, it isn't 99 at all, but 099. So when you write it backwards, write 990. For example:

211 is the number you pick:	**211**
Write it backwards and	
Subtract the smaller number:	**-112**
Total:	**099**
Write it backwards and add it:	**+990**
	1089

The only numbers that won't work are numbers that are written the same backwards and forwards—such as 141, 252, or 343.

HOW OLD ARE YOU?

Try this on your friends:

1. Write down the number of the month in which in which you were born.
2. Multiply by 2.
3. Add 5.
4. Multiply the total by 50.
5. Add the magic number. (The magic number varies from year to year.
    > In 2000 it is 1450;
    > in 2001 it is 1451;
    > in 2002 it is 1452;
    > in 2003 it is 1453, and so on.)
6. Deduct the year you were born.

The last two digits are your age.

THE SECRET: What you're doing in Steps 1–4 is forcing your friends to come up with a figure that ends in the digits 50. Once you have that, and you add the "magic number," the last digits of that figure are the digits of the current year. Then it is a simple matter of deducting the year of birth and coming up with your age. For instance:

Your birth month:	7	
Multiply by 2	= 14	
Add 5	= 19	
Multiply by 50	= 950	
Add magic number	<u>1450</u>	(if it's 2000,
	2400	00 is the current
		year)
Deduct the year you		
were born:	<u>1988</u>	
	12	—your age.

THE SECRET NUMBER

People who are good at math won't have much trouble figuring out why this trick works. Others will be mystified completely. Tell your friends that you are going to read the numbers in their minds if they do what you tell them.

Now ask them to think of a number, but not to tell it to you.

Then tell them to double that number (mentally), multiply the sum by 5, and tell you the result. You knock off the zero on the end and the remainder is the secret number.

For instance, your friend may take 7. Doubling makes it 14, and multiplying it by 5 makes 70. Knock off the zero and 7 is your answer.

HOW IS IT DONE: It always works—because doubling the number and then multiplying it by 5 is just the same as multiplying it by 10. When you take off the zero, of course, you have the original number.

MATH MAGIC

With this fascinating trick, you can add large numbers with remarkable speed and accuracy.

Ask your audience to write down 2 rows of figures, each containing 5 digits, such as:

1st row: 3 4 6 5 8
2nd row: 4 6 8 2 9

Now you put down a third row of figures:

3rd row: 5 3 1 7 0

Ask your audience to put down a fourth:

4th row: 6 2 3 5 3

Now you write a fifth row:

5th row: 3 7 6 4 6

Then you look at the figures a moment and write on a small piece of paper, fold the paper and give it to someone in the audience to hold. Then ask the audience to add up the numbers and call out the total. When they figure it out, call for your slip of paper and unfold it. There—for everyone to see—is the correct total!

HOW IT IS DONE: You work your calculations while you are putting down your rows of figures. When you write the third row, make each of your numbers total 9 when added to the number *just above it* in the second row. (Ignore the top row.) In the fifth row, make each number total 9 when added to the number in the fourth row.

Now you can figure out the grand total very quickly from the *first line*: Just subtract 2 from the last number of the first line (8) and place the 2 in front of the first number.

Audience:	3 4 6 5 8
Audience:	4 6 8 2 9
You:	5 3 1 7 0
Audience:	6 2 3 5 3
You:	<u>3 7 6 4 6</u>
Grand Total:	2 3 4 6 5 6

EXCEPTIONS: If the audience writes a first number that ends in either 0 or 1, you need to mentally reverse the first and second row of figures. When you put down the third row, put down numbers that total 9 when added to the numbers in the first row. Ignore the second row until the grand total. Follow the same procedure as usual with the fourth and fifth rows. But figure the grand total by using the second line—subtracting 2 from the last num

Audience:	3 4 6 5 0
Audience:	4 6 9 2 9
You:	6 5 3 4 9
Audience:	6 2 3 5 3
You:	<u>3 7 6 4 6</u>
Grand Total:	2 4 6 9 2 7

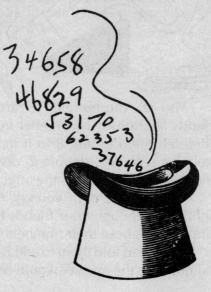

34658
46829
53170
62353
37646

NUMBER WIZARD

You are the number wizard. Ask your friends to choose any number from 1 to 10. Then tell them to add 8 to it in their heads (keeping it secret), double it, divide it by 4, and then subtract half of the original number.

"The answer is 4," you say. And you are right! Even though your friends haven't told you a thing about their numbers.

If you had told them to add 6 to the original number, the answer would be 3.

How does it work? The remainder is always half of the number you tell them to add—everything else cancels out.

Or try this one:

"Take a number," you say. "Add 7, double it, add 16, double again, divide by 4, and subtract 15. Now you each have the number you started with!"

Mystifying? Still it's simple to figure out, because the doubling, dividing, adding and subtracting equal out, and you have really done nothing to change the original number.

MAGIC NUMBER

EQUIPMENT: Paper and pencil for you and your victims.

There actually is a magic number which you can multiply with lightning speed in your head. The number is 142,857. Prepare yourself with paper and pencil and show your friends that the paper is blank. You will use it only to write down the result.

Now give your friends pencils and paper and ask them to multiply 142,857 by any number from 1 to 7. Then ask them, one at a time, to tell you any one figure in the result. Suppose the third figure from the left is 5. You know immediately that the entire total is 285,714! You also know that the multiplier was 2.

Suppose the fourth figure from the left is 4: then you know the total is 571,428 and the multiplier is 4.

Do you get it? Every possible total of this magic number, when multiplied by 1 to 6, results in the same series of digits, but it begins at a different point. Multiply them out if you want to check, or run them through a calculator.

Therefore, if you know the position of any one number in the sequence, you are able to write down the total correctly. In the example, when your friend told you that 4 was the fourth figure, you put down 428 at the end of the total, and 5, 7, and 1 in front, according to the sequence.

How do you know what the number was multiplied by? Look at the last digit you wrote down. Since $4 \times 7 = 28$ (and this is the only combination that ends in an 8) the multiplier gives itself away. That last digit is different for each multiplication.

Oh yes—if you multiply the magic number by 7, you get another magic number:

999,999!

ACROSS

1 "Yo-ho-ho and a bottle of ____"
4 Person who makes up rhymes
8 Unit of computer memory
12 Every once ____ while (2 words)
13 "Hey, what's the big ____?"
14 There might be one on the side of a staircase
15 Game with deeds and Chance cards
17 "Excuse me . . ."
18 That girl
19 Pocket fuzz
21 Word you use during long division
24 You make soup in it
25 Sound of a ray gun
28 Rescue a car
29 Constellations are made up of them
31 Animal that gives birth to lambs
32 "____ was saying . . ." (2 words)
33 Baby goat
34 Vehicle that can handle rough terrain
35 Part of the leg
37 Sticky stuff
39 ____ Rose (famous ballplayer who was banned from baseball)
41 Game with tiles and Triple Letter Squares
46 "And they lived happily ____ after"
47 Fix mistakes in writing
48 Younger version of the word in 3-Down
49 "What ____ we thinking?"
50 Part of a camera
51 Take someone to court

DOWN

1 It surrounds a basketball net
2 Numero ____ (#1)
3 Guy
4 Frosty the Snowman had one
5 Bad smell
6 Long, skinny fish
7 Jonathan ____ Thomas
8 Ingredient in some cereals that has a lot of fiber
9 Game with dice and "small straights"
10 Make a knot
11 Kind of tree
16 Exclamation like "Aha!"
20 "____ none of your business!"

#1

21 "Give ____ chance!"
   (2 words)
22 1, 2, and 3: Abbreviation
23 Game with colored
   circles and a spinner
24 Lily ____ (what a frog
   sits on)
26 In ____ of (impressed by)
27 ____ rally
29 Glide down a snowy
   mountain
30 Shiny stuff on a
   Christmas tree
34 What someone does

for a living
36 In this spot
37 Smile broadly
38 Grains that horses eat
39 Long seat in church
40 Christmas ____
   (December 24)
42 Letters between B and F
43 Ammo for a toy gun
44 "Skip to My ____"
45 Private ____ (detective)

Answer on page 324

59

ACROSS

1 Dog, cat, or hamster, for example
4 Emergency letters
7 Jewish religious leader
12 "I ____ you one!"
13 Wolf down
14 Tim ____ ("Home Improvement" star)
15 Comic strip by Charles Schultz
17 Football team in Detroit
18 Suffix for "heir"
19 "____ sesame!"
20 Walks in water
23 Word that Scrooge said
24 When the sun is out
27 ____ rain (ecology problem)
28 Miles ____ hour
29 Drink that's made in Napa Valley
30 Kind of toothpaste
31 What groceries are put into
32 You pull them out of a garden
33 It comes at the end of a restaurant meal
35 You need it for frying
36 Birds that fly in a V-shape
38 Comic strip by Bill Amend
42 Monsters in fairy tales
43 Get older
44 "What ____ you talking about?"
45 Carries
46 ____ and reel
47 Ballpoint ____

DOWN

1 The sound a balloon makes
2 Female sheep
3 The Mad Hatter drank it
4 Dr. ____ (children's book author)
5 Some grains
6 Roads: Abbreviation
7 Character on "Happy Days"
8 Tell ____ (fib): 2 words
9 Comic strip by Chic Young
10 Big ____ (famous landmark in London)
11 Drive-____ (places where movies are watched from cars)
16 Require
19 It helps row a boat
20 What a dog's tail might do
21 "Ace ____, Pet Detective"
22 Comic strip by Scott Adams
23 Plead
25 Hide- ____ -seek

#2

26 Word of agreement
28 Good friend
29 "They ____ thataway!"
31 "____ you!" (reaction to a sneeze)
32 Polished the floor
34 "Peekaboo, ____ you! (2 words)
35 ____ stick (bouncy toy)
36 "You've ____ to be kidding"
37 What a conceited person has a lot of

38 Distant
39 Kind of music Queen Latifah makes
40 Raw metal
41 A dozen minus a pair

Answer on page 324

ACROSS

1 Boxer's punches
5 Cooio's music
8 Big wooden pole on a ship
12 Words of understanding: (2 words)
13 Suffix that means "most"
14 State that has a lot of Mormons
15 Disney movie
17 Not early
18 "What ____ doing here?" (2 words)
19 Health resort
21 "____ the season to be jolly . . ."
24 "Oh, what's the ____?" ("What difference does it make?")
26 Vegetable that makes you cry when you chop it
30 Stuff in a pen
31 Look without blinking
33 Number in a duo
34 Perhaps
36 Decay
37 Do what Betsy Ross was famous for doing
38 Commercials
40 Get ready to shoot a basketball
42 Not quite hot
45 Disney movie
50 Someone who lives in the Middle East
51 "____ got an idea!"
52 Final
53 Prefix for "colon" or "final"
54 Homer's neighbor on "The Simpsons"
55 Potatoes have them

DOWN

1 Brand of peanut butter
2 Red ____ beet: (2 words)
3 "Boy Meets World" actor Savage
4 ____ good example (what a role model should do): (2 words)
5 "I couldn't ____" ("I just had to do it")
6 "Do ____ say!": (2 words)
7 School groups that have open houses: Abbreviation
8 Disney movie
9 One ____ time (2 words)
10 Got into a chair
11 Most commonly written word in English
16 Made other people laugh
20 Like something written in verse
21 Tiny ____ (character in "A Christmas Carol")

#3

22 "Never ____ million years!" (2 words)
23 Where clouds are
25 Hearing organ
27 "____ been real!" ("I've had fun!")
28 Homophone of "oh"
29 At this moment
32 Sounded like a lion
35 Disney movie
39 ____ guards (protection for soccer players)
41 Stubborn animal

42 The past tense of "is"
43 "We ____ the World"
44 Male sheep
46 New Year's ____
47 Put down
48 Ending for "Japan" or "Vietnam"
49 Roads: Abbreviation

Answer on page 324

ACROSS

1 Big crowd
4 Drink that contains caffeine
7 Raises up _____
12 Kwik-E-Mart worker on "The Simpsons"
13 Like the numbers 3, 11, and 19
14 Really love
15 Woman who is half fish
17 Noisy thing on a fire truck
18 _____ Frank (famous diary writer)
19 Half of twenty
21 The _____ Sea (body of water bordering Israel)
22 Celebrity
24 Short swim
26 Roads and avenues: Abbreviations
27 Command to a dog
29 _____ office (place to mail letters)
31 "Do _____ say!": (2 words)
33 Diamond or ruby, for example
35 Makes a ditch
37 Singer who used to be married to Sonny Bono
39 Money left for a waitress
41 Got bigger
43 Bees make it

45 Not in any place
47 Bert and _____ ("Sesame Street" friends)
48 Part of the foot
49 Woman in the Garden of Eden
50 People in charge of colleges
51 Pronoun for a woman
52 _____ Flanders (character on "The Simpsons")

DOWN

1 Baby's first word, sometimes
2 Unlocks
3 Crayola color: (2 words)
4 "One _____ customer": (2 words)
5 Make changes in an article
6 Did sums
7 _____ Vegas, Nevada
8 "_____ it!" (successful shout): (2 words)
9 Crayola color: (2 words)
10 "Trick or _____"
11 Puts in the mail
16 Hamburger or chicken, for example
20 Little bite
23 Old piece of cloth
25 It contains peas
28 So far

#4

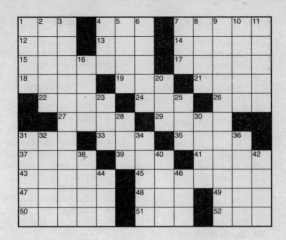

30 Make an "Oh Well!" sound
31 Felt sore all over
32 Area next to the ocean
34 After-dinner ____ (breath-freshening candies)
36 Start a game of tennis
38 Strap that controls a horse
40 Winnie-the-____
42 Plant that you don't want in a garden

44 Word of agreement
46 Pee-____ Herman

Answer on page 324

ACROSS

1 "The Red Planet"
5 One day ____ time: (2 words)
8 Conversation
12 State where Toledo is
13 Stimpy's pal, in cartoons
14 Bart Simpson's sister
15 Bundles of paper
16 Enemies of Batman
18 "Just ____!" (Nike's slogan): (2 words)
20 Use a needle and thread
21 Good buddy
23 Small bite
25 Enter data for a computer
29 People shout it to the bullfighter
30 Scrub really hard
32 Ending for "Japan"
33 Winter coat
35 Conclusion
36 One of the Bobbsey Twins
37 "Jack ____ Jill"
39 ____ Island (part of New York)
41 Enemy of Batman: (2 words, Abbreviation)
45 Uncle's wife
48 Part for an actor
49 They're not yeses

50 Chest protectors for babies
51 Graceful bird
52 Letters that signal for help
53 Metal fastener

DOWN

1 Clean the floor
2 "I knew it!"
3 Enemy of Batman
4 Just okay: Hyphenated
5 Ocean near the North Pole
6 Drink that's made from leaves
7 Little bugs
8 Bozo or Ronald McDonald
9 That guy
10 White ____ sheet: (2 words)
11 Slightly brown
17 Strange person
19 Crazy
21 " ____ Goes the Weasel"
22 ____ mode (with ice cream): (2 words)
24 Edgar Allan ____ (famous writer)
26 Enemy of Batman
27 Country between Canada and Mexico: Abbreviation
28 Number of arms on a squid

66

31 "Don't do anything
_____ I tell you to"
34 Girl's name
38 Comfortable rooms in
houses
40 Captures
41 Abbreviation before a
wife's name
42 Move a canoe
43 Miami's state:
Abbreviation
44 Place to see animals

46 Shaquille O'Neal's
group:
Abbreviation
47 ¹/₂ of a tablespoon:
Abbreviation

Answer on page 325

ACROSS

1 Sinks downward
5 Supposed ability to read minds: Abbreviation
8 Cool ____ cucumber: (2 words)
11 Sign above a door, sometimes
12 Thin as a ____
14 Corny joke
15 "If it ____ up to me . . ."
16 Zoo animal
18 Planet of the ____"
20 ____ shoes (things a ballerina wears)
21 Not on
23 The square root of 100
25 They're sold by the dozen
29 TV alien from the planet Melmac
30 Stuffed-____ pizza
33 Big tree
34 Sandwich breads
36 Pekoe is a type of this
37 Baseball statistic: Abbreviation
38 Sam-____ (Dr. Suess character): Hyphenated
41 Me, myself, ____: (2 words)
43 Zoo animal
47 Too

50 "____ and improved"
51 Captain Hook's sidekick in "Peter Pan"
52 Cole ____ (common side dish)
53 Opposite of "live"
54 Put two and two together
55 Detest

DOWN

1 Join with stitches
2 The Tin Man carried one
3 Zoo animal
4 A ____ in the right direction
5 One end of a pencil
6 ____ Francisco
7 Movie star Brad ____
8 "Many years ____ . . ."
9 It comes out of maple trees
10 Ending for "orphan" or "percent"
13 Zodiac sign that comes after Cancer
17 Grant's opponent in the Civil War
19 "And others": Abbreviation
21 Paddle for a boat
22 Go up in a plane
24 Cashew or macadamia
26 Zoo animal
27 Talk and talk and talk
28 Water- ____ (have fun on a lake)

#6

31 "Please be ____" ("Get in your chairs")

32 Light brown color

35 Take a tiny drink of

39 Sounds the doctor tells you to make

40 One of the Berenstain Bears

42 Hundred-yard ____ (kind of race)

43 "____ of the Road" (Boyz II Men song)

44 Ring of flowers they give out on Hawaii

45 She gives birth to a lamb

46 Boy's name

48 Weekend day: Abbreviation

49 "I ____ you one!" ("I'm in your debt!")

Answer on page 325

ACROSS

1 It forms on top of a wound
5 Janitors use them
9 Tiny ____ ("A Christmas Carol" character)
12 Part of a golf course
13 Tell ____ (don't tell the truth): (2 words)
14 Astonishment
15 Ending for "respect"
16 Place, like on the internet
17 Amount at an auction
18 Ice cream flavor: (2 words)
21 Shade of brown
22 It lives in a hive
23 Room in a prison
24 Ending for "count" or "baron"
25 "Mighty ____ Young" (movie about a gorilla)
27 Separate with a sieve
30 2000 pounds
31 Music recordings, for short
34 Ice cream flavor: (2 words)
38 X-____ vision (one of Superman's powers)
39 Direction on a compass
40 Green citrus fruit

41 Munched on
42 Not early
43 Last word of a prayer
44 What the P stands for in "MPH"
45 Moved quickly
46 Annoying person

DOWN

1 The long, thin part of an arrow
2 Snake that has a hood
3 Woody ____ (famous movie director)
4 "Where have you ____?"
5 Makes potatoes ready for eating
6 ____ Oyl (Popeye's girlfriend)
7 Bread that has a pocket
8 Looked at
9 Kitchen furniture
10 "____ Always Love You" (Whitney Houston song): (2 words)
11 What an Olympic winner gets
19 One of the TV networks
20 Cubes that are in the freezer
24 "And on and on": Abbreviation

70

#7

25 Wrote down in a hurry
26 Half of two
27 ____ heap (pile of junk)
28 " ____ you!" ("You're not my friend anymore!"): (2 words)
29 Area near the front door, in some houses
30 Try the food
31 Wind ____ (thing that hangs outside and makes jingly sounds)
32 Ten-cent coins
33 Used cash
35 Nighttime birds with big eyes
36 Jump
37 Applaud

Answer on page 325

ACROSS

1 "Get ____ my back!"
4 Joint near the middle of the body
7 Command a dog learns in obedience school
11 ____ Blanc (person who did the voice of Bugs Bunny)
12 They go on kings or twos in the card game spit
14 State where Cincinnati is
15 "Prince ____" (song in the movie "Aladdin")
16 You go camping in one
17 Person who's not cool
18 Presses on a horn
20 "I'm ____ kidding!"
22 The Mediterranean ____
23 Prefix for "gravity" or "freeze"
24 Big structure in Egypt
26 Five-pointed thing
28 Important test
29 Home music systems
31 Health resorts
34 "____ says so?"
35 It's used to make roads
36 Copy of a magazine
37 ____ and rave (argue loudly)
39 Word that appears on the thing at 6-down

41 Kind of poem (homophone for "owed")
42 Like the numbers 2, 4, and 6
43 Tools for gardeners
44 Tiny nibble
45 What a bird builds
46 Place for a pig
47 "Help us!"

DOWN

1 Big city in Nebraska
2 Criminal
3 Cartoon set in caveman times, with "The"
4 Head coverings
5 Put frosting on a cake
6 Small coin
7 Father's boy
8 Cartoon set in Springfield: (2 words)
9 Showed on television, for example
10 Wise creature in the "Star Wars" films
13 Shopping places
19 "Go fly a ____!"
21 What the Internal Revenue Service collects
24 "Practice what you ____!"
25 Boston's state: Abbreviation
27 Paintings and so on

#8

29 Get rid of a beard
30 Cookies with white middles
32 Word that can go before "visual"
33 Oozes
34 Small brown bird
36 "The _____ -Bitsy Spider"
38 Stuff that can cause an explosion: Abbreviation
40 A fisherman might throw it into the water

Answer on page 325

ACROSS

1 What keys fit into
6 " ____ my pleasure"
9 Get at a store
12 Musical that includes the song "Tomorrow"
13 "How ____ you?"
14 Sly ____ fox: 2 words
15 Kriss Kringle's other name
16 Mother
17 Uncle ____ (symbol of America
18 Word that might end a list: Abbreviation
20 Little ____ Muffet
22 Work in the movies
25 Big chunk of something
27 "I made a mistake!"
30 ____ of (in a way)
32 A while ____ (in the past)
33 Someone who isn't interesting
34 What the "big hand" points to
35 Some people pay it every month
37 "Do ____ Pass Go . . ." (phrase in the game Monopoly)
38 It can go before "skirt" or "van"
40 You might get it pierced

42 ____ code (number at the end of an address)
44 Now ____ then
46 The end of one of Aesop's Fables
50 Card with just one symbol on it
51 Split ____ soup
52 Run away to get married
53 " ____ out of here!"
54 Messy place
55 Did some stitching

DOWN

1 ____ Vegas
2 "I'm ____ roll!" ("Nothing is going wrong!"): 2 words
3 TV channel that shows mostly news
4 Toy that has a long tail
5 Chairs
6 "Do you know who ____ ?": 2 words
7 Orchestra instrument
8 Prefix for "finals" or "annual"
9 Orchestra instrument
10 Country formed in 1776: Abbreviation
11 Vegetable also called a sweet potato
19 Orchestra instrument

74

#9

21 Weep loudly
22 What's left after something is burned
23 Sound a pigeon makes
24 Orchestra instrument
26 Number of years you've been around
28 ____ wrestling (Hulk Hogan's sport)
29 All ____ (ready to go)
31 Beginning for "cycle"
36 Makes less wild
39 Takes a short sleep

41 Part in a play
42 Zig and ____
43 Skating surface
45 24 hours
47 Pull on the oars
48 Monkey's big relative
49 Didn't follow

Answer on page 325

CARD TRICKS

THE TWO ROWS

THE EFFECT: You tell a spectator—say, Geoff—to deal two rows of cards, each row containing the same number of cards, so that he'll have the number firmly fixed in his mind.

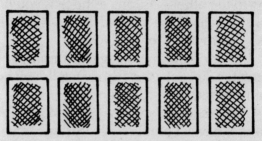

He can use any number of cards in each row from 3 or 4 to 20; it is entirely up to him. You are going to give him instructions on how to rearrange the rows in various ways. While he is rearranging them, you either turn your back or go into another room (as long as he can hear you from there).

When Geoff is ready, tell him to take away cards from either row, but to state *how many* cards he takes, and from which row.

When he does that, tell him he can do what he wants— take more cards from either row—or add cards, or transfer them from one row to the other—as long as he tells you how many cards were moved and says which row—or rows—are involved.

At one point, you suggest a number for Geoff to take away, but he never tells you how many cards either row contains.

Then suddenly you say, "Stop!" And you name the exact number of cards that remain.

HOW IT IS DONE: The number of cards in each row does not matter, as long as they are equal at the start. For example, assume that Geoff puts 7 cards in each row:

TOP: * * * * * * *
BOTTOM: * * * * * * *

You don't see these cards, but you take a high number of your own—say 20—and imagine or visualize the rows as containing 20 cards each. Then you ask Geoff to take away cards, add them, or move them as he chooses, but to tell you what he does. Like this:

He moves 3 cards from the bottom row to the top, and says so. That leaves:

TOP: * * * * * * * * * *
BOTTOM: * * * *

Working from your "key" number 20, you mentally move 3 from bottom to top, saying to yourself: "Twenty-three in the top row—17 in the bottom row."

Now, suppose Geoff takes away 2 from the bottom row, stating that fact. He has:

TOP: * * * * * * * * * *
BOTTOM: * *

You say to yourself: "Two from 17 leaves 15 in the bottom row—23 still in the top."

Geoff decides to add one card to each row, so that the rows stand:

TOP: * * * * * * * * * * *
BOTTOM: * * *

Mentally, you add one to each of your rows, giving you 24 in the top row and 16 in the bottom row.

Now comes the important part: You tell Geoff to count the number of cards in the bottom row and take that many away from the top row. He takes 3 (the number in his bottom row) from the 11 cards in his top row, which gives him:

TOP: * * * * * * * *
BOTTOM: * * *

Meanwhile, you do the same with your

imaginary rows, subtracting 16 (bottom) from 24 (top) so you have 8 cards in your top row.

Then you tell Geoff to take away his entire bottom row, leaving him with a single row:

* * * * * * * *

You too eliminate your imaginary bottom row (16 cards), and that leaves you with a single row of just 8 cards, identical with the row now on the table!

From then on, you can let Geoff add or subtract cards as he wants, providing he states the exact number in each case. You go right along with him, for you are both working with the same number.

Assume that he simply takes away 4 cards. He then has:

* * * *

You do the same and announce your final total: "Four!"

MUTUS DEDIT NOMEN COCIS

THE EFFECT: Give the spectator—Sally Ann—a packet of 20 cards to lay out on the table *facedown* in sets of two. Then turn your back and ask her to select one of these sets of two, look at the cards in it, and remember them.

Other spectators can look at a set, too. If there are ten people watching, each one can look at a set of two and remember it.

Turning around now, you gather up the sets, keeping them together, and lay the cards out on the table *face up* in four rows of 5 cards each.

"Which one or two rows are your cards in?" you ask Sally Ann.

As soon as she points to the rows which house her two cards, you announce what they are. And you do the same thing for any other spectators who point out the rows their two cards are in.

HOW IT IS DONE: This trick is based on code words, which you need to memorize. The words are "Mutus" (pronounced MEW-tus), "Dedit" (DEAD-it), "Nomen" (NO-mun), "Cocis" (COCK-us).

M U T U S	1	2	3	2	4
D E D I T	5	6	5	7	3
N O M E N	8	9	1	6	8
C O C I S	10	9	10	7	4

When you lay out the cards, instead of just putting them down in any old order, you follow the letter pattern in the words. For example, you put the first set (two cards) down in the spots occupied by the M's—the M in Mutus and the only other M spot, the M in Nomen. Then you put the second set of two cards into the spots reserved for the U's—both of them in Mutus. And so on for set #3: start with the T in Mutus; then go to the T in Dedit, and so on until you have laid out all the sets.

So when you ask Sally Ann to point out the rows (horizontally) in which her cards are located, it is a simple question of finding the two identical letters.

If Sally Ann says both cards are in the first row, you know automatically that it is the set of U's in Mutus. If they are in rows 1 and 2, you know she had the T's in Mutus and Dedit. If they are in rows 1 and 3, she had the M's in Mutus and Nomen. If they are in rows 1 and 4, she had the S positions in Mutus and Cocis.

If the cards are only in the second row, she had the D's in Dedit. If they are in the second and third rows, she had the E's in Dedit and Nomen. If they are in the second and last rows, they are the I's in Dedit and Cocis.

If Sally Ann says her cards are only in the third row, she had the N's in Nomen. In the third and fourth rows, she had the O's in Nomen and Cocis. And if they are just in the last row, she had the C's in Cocis.

T A R O T

E N D E R

I O N I C

S C A D S

Here are three other arrangements:

S A L A D

Z I P P S

M O T O R

S H E E R

N I N T H

M I L L S

T I T L E

O O Z E D

DO AS I DO

This classic trick will really bewilder your audience, but it is easy to do once you learn to handle the cards in a convincing way.

THE EFFECT: You take two packs of cards and let a spectator—say, Joyce—choose either pack. You shuffle one pack, and she shuffles the other.

To show that all is fair, you then exchange packs, so that each of you shuffles the other's. Finally, you hand your pack to Joyce and say, "From now on, do as I do, and let's see what happens."

You deal your pack in three heaps on the table. Joyce does the same thing with her pack.

You lift the top card of the middle heap and peek at it. Joyce does the same, and you remind her, "I am remembering my card, so I want you to remember yours."

Now you gather the heaps and give your pack two or three cuts. Joyce does the same with her pack. Remarking that the peeked-at cards are now "well buried," you exchange packs again. Then you say:

"I am going to look through your pack and take out the card that I found in mine. You look through my pack and find yours. Then we'll put them facedown on the table."

Once you each pick out your cards, set the packs aside. Dramatically, you turn up the two cards. They are identical! By an amazing coincidence, you have each taken the same card from a different pack!

HOW IT IS DONE: After a few shuffles and exchanges, take a peek at the bottom card of the pack that you hand to Joyce. Here is one way to do it:

Let's say the bottom card is the 9 of Clubs. You take her pack and say:
"Now do as I do."

Lift off about ⅔ of the pack, and set it to the right. Then lift off the top third and set it out further to the right.

Joyce does the same with the pack.

Peek at the top card of the middle heap, but don't bother to remember it. Keep thinking of that bottom card of the other pack. Pick up the left-hand heap of your pack, put it on the middle heap, and place both heaps on the top heap.

Joyce does the same with her pack. In the process, she plants the bottom card—the 9 of Clubs that you secretly noted—squarely on the card at which she peeked!

You cut the pack two or three times, and chances are the two cards will remain together. So after you exchange packs again, simply look through Joyce's pack for the 9 of Clubs, and remove the card just below it, say the Jack of Diamonds.

That will be the card she looked at. Meanwhile, she is looking through your pack, finding the Jack of Diamonds and taking it out as you instructed. So the two cards turn out to be identical.

FOUR-HEAP DEAL

THE EFFECT: You shuffle the deck thoroughly and spread it *facedown* on the table so that a spectator—say, Jennifer—can remove any four cards, which she lays down in a row.

Gather up the pack and hand it to Jennifer. Then turn your back and tell her to turn up the first of the four cards and note its value: 1 for Ace, 2 for deuce, and so on. All face cards (Jacks, Queens and Kings) count 10.

On that first card, Jennifer deals enough additional cards *(facedown)* to total 12. For example, on a 7 she would deal five cards, on a 10 or a King, two cards.

Now Jennifer turns up the next card in the row and repeats the process, and continues with the third and fourth cards. Here is a sample result:

Now you tell Jennifer to count down into the pack and turn up the card which is the total of all the faceup cards. She is to look at it and remember it. Then you call out the name of a card, say "Queen of Hearts," and it proves to be the chosen card.

HOW IT IS DONE: You need a pack of exactly 52 cards, so remove any Jokers beforehand. All you have to do is get a look at the bottom card after the shuffle—in this case, the Queen of Hearts—the rest is automatic.

For example, if 4 Aces were turned up, Jennifer would deal 11 cards on each, making 48 in all. Only 4 cards would be left in the pack. She would gather the 44 facedown cards, drop the 4 cards from the pack on top and count down the total of the Aces, exactly 4 cards.

With four 10's or face cards, she would deal 2 on each, making 8 facedown cards and leaving 40 cards in the pack. She would gather up the 8 cards, drop the rest of the pack on top and count down the value of the 10's (or face cards), which would come to 40.

Tell Jennifer she can gather the facedown heaps in any order she wants and place the rest of the pack facedown on the pile. Tell her to add the totals of the faceup cards. In the example (page 92), the cards would add up to 27.

THE MULTIPLYING CARDS

EQUIPMENT: A flat plate
20 playing cards

THE EFFECT: One by one you place about 10 cards on a flat plate and ask a member of the audience to count them. The volunteer does this and returns the cards to the table, but you shake your head and look doubtful. Then you ask another volunteer to check the number of cards once more. You personally hand the volunteer the cards. To everyone's surprise, there turn out to be twice as many cards as before!

HOW IT IS DONE: The illustration gives the trick away. You have hidden the extra cards under the plate. You hold them in place with your right hand, which is holding the plate. Using your left hand, you push the cards on top of the plate under your right thumb, and with your left hand, you take the plate, uniting the two piles. Throughout this procedure, hold the plate at a slight angle forward so that no one can see the pile of cards under the plate.

It will be very easy to pick up both the plate and the concealed pile of cards at the same time if you place them both at the very edge of the table, with the edge of the cards overhanging the table, in fact.

DOUBLE DEAL

This trick is based upon a neat but simple mathematical stunt, and it becomes a real puzzler when you allow the spectators to mystify themselves.

THE EFFECT: Give Dorothy a pack of cards and tell her to deal off any number up to 20 while your back is turned. When she does that, tell her to deal another heap with the same number of cards—to make sure she doesn't forget that number.

Then tell her to deal a third heap of 10 cards, gather all the heaps together, and deal them into two separate piles, alternating left and right. Dorothy then is to pick up either pile. From it she deals the original number of cards onto the other heap.

Finally, Dorothy counts the remaining cards in her hand and concentrates on that number. You immediately announce the number of cards she is holding.

And the entire trick is done with your back to the audience.

HOW IT IS DONE: The trick hinges on the third heap of cards you tell Dorothy to deal, the pile of ten. At the finish, she will have just half that number, so by announcing "Five," you are sure to be correct.

For example, suppose Dorothy deals 8 cards. Told to deal the same number again, she deals 8 more, making 16. Now you say, "Deal 10 more." That brings the total to 26.

Then Dorothy deals the cards into two heaps that will contain just 13 cards each. From one of these, she deals the original number—8—into the other. That leaves exactly 5 cards, the number you proceed to name.

Note: When you repeat the trick, change the number you tell her to deal. If you tell her to deal 6 more, the final total will be 3. If you tell her to deal 12 more, the total will be 6, and so on.

CARD GAMES for One

FOUR-LEAF CLOVER

You will have good luck all day if you win this game—they say.

Discard all four 10's from the deck. You won't be using them at all. Shuffle the remaining 48 cards well. Then deal 16 cards faceup on the table in four rows of four cards each.

Whenever you can, throw out from these rows any two or more cards of the same suit. These can be (a) two or more cards that total 15 each, such as 9 and 6 or 8, 4, 2, and Ace (Ace counts 1); (b) three cards, the King, Queen and Jack.

After you throw out a batch of cards, deal from the deck to fill the spaces left in the 16-card layout.

TO WIN THE GAME: You must throw out all 48 cards (deal out the whole deck).

THE CAVE MAN GAME
(No More Clubs)

Discard all 2's to 6's, leaving a deck of 32 cards. Shuffle them well and then deal three cards faceup in a column at your left. If any one of them is a Club, throw it out to start a waste pile. Then deal a new card to take its place. If the new card is a Club, throw it out and deal another—and so on—until you have three non-Clubs in the column.

Then deal four more columns of three cards each, from left to right. From this array of 15 cards, throw all the Clubs into the waste pile.

Gather the cards again (except for the Clubs that you threw out), and shuffle them together. Deal a second time in the same way as the first, and again throw out all the Clubs. Then gather the remaining cards, shuffle again, and deal a third time.

TO WIN THE GAME: You must discard all eight Clubs in the three deals.

HIT CARDS

Deal the cards one at a time faceup into a single waste pile. As you deal, count "Ace, two, three, four . . ." and so on up to the King. Whenever the card you deal is the same as the rank you call, it's a hit! Throw all the "hit" cards out of the deck. After you count "King," start over again with "Ace, two . . ." and so on. When you have dealt the entire deck, pick up the waste pile, turn it facedown, and continue dealing. Also continue counting, from where you left off.

TO WIN THE GAME: You must hit every card in the deck. But you lose if you go through the deck twice in a row without a single hit.

ACCORDION

Deal the cards one at a time faceup, in a row of 4 from left to right. Go slowly so that you can keep comparing the cards you deal with their neighbors. Whenever a card matches its immediate neighbor at the left, or the card third to its left, you move the new card over onto the one it matches. The matching may be in suit or rank.

Suppose that the first four cards you turn up are:

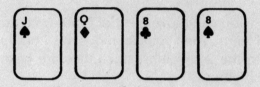

The 8 of Spades matches the 8 of Clubs and also the Jack of Spades. You may move it over upon either card. Here it is just a guess which play will turn out better. Later on, you will find that one play is better than another, when you have a choice, because it opens additional plays. Keep watching for new plays you make possible when you consolidate piles.

For example, suppose that you deal:

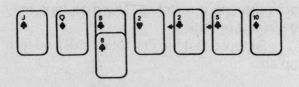

You can move the 2 of Clubs onto the 2 of Hearts. Then you can move the 5 of Clubs onto the 2 of Clubs, since they are next to each other.

Move the entire pile of cards—not just the top card. When you create a gap in a row because you moved a pile away, shove all the piles leftward to close up the gap.

TO WIN THE GAME: You must get the whole deck into one pile. You won't succeed very often. You really can consider it a win if you end up with 5 piles or less.

THE CLOCK

Shuffle the deck, and then deal it into 13 piles of four cards each, all facedown.

Arrange 12 of the piles in a circle, to represent the numbers on a clock dial. Put the thirteenth pile in the middle of the circle. Start by picking up the top card of the thirteenth pile. Suppose it is a 5. Shove it faceup under the 5-pile and pick up the top card of the 5-pile. Suppose it is a Queen. Put it under the 12-pile and pick up the top of the 12-pile—and so on.

Jacks represent 11, Queens 12, Kings 13; other cards have their spot value.

TO WIN THE GAME: You must get all the cards faceup. You lose if you come to the fourth King before all the other cards have been moved faceup to their proper hour piles.

PYRAMID

Lay the cards out in the shape of a pyramid.
Start with one card at the top, overlap it with
the next two cards, then overlap these with
three cards, and so on until you have a large
triangle with seven cards at the base.

Each card has its own numerical value:

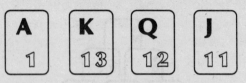

Your job is to remove all the cards that add up to 13 (two at a time), with this catch: you cannot remove a card unless it is "open"—not covered by any other card.

For example, in the pyramid (page 109), you can remove the 9 and the 4, and the Jack (11) and the 2 from the bottom row. This opens up the King and Queen of Hearts in the next row. You can remove the King, because he counts as 13 by himself. You can also remove the Queen (12) and the Ace (1).

Place all the cards you remove in a discard pile, faceup. The top card in this pile can be used again to form another 13-match. Right now, the top card is an Ace. You can match it with the Queen of Diamonds, which is still in the pyramid, and remove that.

Now you start dealing out the rest of the pack, one by one. If you cannot make a match with the card that you turn up, start a separate "discard" pile. Don't mix up this pile with your "removed" pile! In order to win the game, you need to dispose not only of the whole pyramid, but of the cards in your hand as well! You get two redeals (three times through the deck) to give you the opportunity to do it.

Let's say the next usable card that comes along is the 3 of Spades. You could use it to match up with one of the 10's which are open in the pyramid. As Kings come up from the deck, you can put them in the "removed" pile automatically.

The second time you go through the cards in your hand, you have some idea of their order, and that should help you plan and scheme a little to clear away additional cards from the pyramid and from your hand.

HOW TO SCORE: A match is six games. Score each game individually as follows:

50 points— **if you get rid of your pyramid in the first deal (once through the cards in the deck). From that score, deduct one point for each card left in the deck. You get two more deals anyway to reduce the number of cards in the deck.**

35 points— **if you get rid of the pyramid during the second deal, after deducting one point for each card left in the deck (you get another deal to reduce that number).**

20 points— **if you get rid of the pyramid on the third deal, after deducting one point for each card left in the deck.**

0 points— if you never do succeed in getting rid of your pyramid, after deducting one point for each card left in the pyramid, and deducting one point for each card left in the deck. That's right, a minus score.

"Par" is 0 for 6 matches. If you do better, you've won!

MY MUMMY TAUGHT ME THIS GAME!

GAPS

Deal out the whole deck faceup in four rows of 13 cards each. Pick out the four Aces and put them aside, leaving gaps in the rows. Examine the card to the left of each gap. The next-higher card of the same suit may be moved into the gap.

For example, if the 8 of Diamonds is to the left of a gap, you may fill the gap with the 9 of Diamonds. This leaves a gap—which you fill in with the card that is one rank higher than the card to the left of the gap.

Whenever you create a gap at the left end of a row, fill it with any 2 that you please.

TO WIN THE GAME: You must get all four suits in order, one in each row, from 2 to King, going from left to right.

When a King lies to the left of a gap, that gap is dead; you cannot fill it. Usually, all four gaps go dead after a while. Then gather up all the cards except the Aces and the cards that are in proper sequence with a 2 at the left end of a row.

Shuffle the cards well; deal them again to remake the four rows of 13, leaving a gap in each row just to the right of the cards that were not gathered up. That allows you to bring one additional card into its proper place on each row, to start you on a new series of plays.

When you are blocked again, gather and redeal the cards in the same way. You are allowed three deals in all.

THE WISH

If you win this game the first time you try it, you will get your wish—so they say.

Use a deck of 32 cards, as in "The Caveman Game." Shuffle them well and then count off four cards at a time *facedown*. Then turn them *faceup*. Be careful to keep the pile squared up so that you cannot see what any of the cards are below the top.

Deal the whole deck into piles of four cards in the same way.

Then lift off the top cards in pairs of the same kind—two 7's, two Queens, and so on. Keep going as long as you see any pairs.

TO WIN THE GAME: You must clear away all the cards in pairs.

PERPETUAL MOTION

Deal four cards faceup in a row from left to right. If any of them are of the same rank (6's, Aces, Kings, etc.) move them onto the one farthest to the left.

Then deal four more cards from left to right on the four piles (count a space as a pile if you moved any of the first four cards). Play in the same way, if you can, moving two or more cards of the same rank upon the leftmost card of that rank. Make all these moves one card (the top card) at a time. Do not move a whole pile at a time.

Continue dealing the deck, four cards at a time on the previous piles, making what moves you can each time.

When you have used up the deck, pick up the piles from right to left. That is, put pile #4 (at the right), still faceup, on pile #3 (at its left). Put them together on pile #2 and then put the whole bunch on pile #1. Don't get the cards mixed up.

Then turn the whole pile facedown, forming a new stock. Go through it again in the same way. You may deal out the stock this way any number of times, until you finally win the game or are blocked.

Whenever the four cards you deal at one time prove to be of the same rank, throw all four cards out, reducing the size of the stock.

TO WIN THE GAME: Throw out the entire deck in batches of four of a rank.

KLONDIKE

Lay out seven cards in a row, facedown, except for the first card. Then put card #8 faceup squarely on top of the second card in the row, and lay down another layer of facedown cards, one for every pile you've started. Then put a faceup card on the third pile, and finish off the row with a layer of facedown cards. Continue in this way until you have a faceup card on every pile.

**These are the
facedown cards
beneath the faceup cards**

Your layout will look like this:

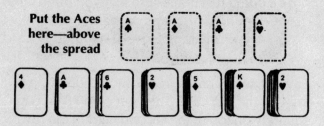

**Put the Aces
here—above
the spread**

Now you are ready to play.

First, look over the spread carefully. You can move a card if:

1. It is an Ace. Put it up above the spread. This is a "point."

2. It is a Deuce of the same suit as an Ace that you put up (another point).

3. It follows the deuce, since you are going to be building up complete sets of each suit up at the top, starting with the Aces and going all the way to the Kings (if you can). Make sure there are no threes and fours or any other

cards you can put up. Every one of them will be a point. Just make sure that you build each Ace-to-King with cards of the same suit.

4. It is one rank lower than another card in the layout and of a different color. For instance, if you have a 9 of Hearts and an 8 of Clubs faceup in the spread, you can move the 8 of Clubs onto the 9 of Hearts, leaving the top of the 9 showing. If a 10 of Spades (or Clubs) opens up, you can move the 9 onto it.

Every time you move a card from the spread onto another card, you "open up" a new card. It could be an Ace, which you can put at the top, or another scoring card, or it might be a card that will help you open up another card somewhere else. The more cards you open up, the closer you are to winning the game. If there is no facedown card under the card that you move, you have a vacant column, and you can move a King—but only a King—into it.

When you're sure there are no further moves you can make from the layout, you start turning over cards, one by one, from the rest of the deck. Study the spread carefully before deciding you can't use the card, because you won't get another chance at it. You can only go through the deck once.

Keep a sharp eye on the sets that you are building at the top, so that you don't miss any cards that fit into them.

When you have finished going through the cards, the game is over. The cards you have managed to place up at the top are your points. Five rounds of Klondike make a game and give you your total score.

Some people don't go through the cards one by one, but instead count them off in threes. If you choose the counting-off-by-threes method, you can go through the deck as many times as you want.

CANFIELD

A shorter, faster game than Klondike, Canfield is played much the same way, but it starts from a different basic layout.

For Canfield, count out 13 cards into one packet and put them in front of you *faceup* and a little to the left. These 13 cards become a sort of "bank" from which you draw new cards to play with.

Then lay out a row of four cards, faceup.

Check the four-card spread carefully to see whether you can make any moves within it. You can't put any cards on the 13-pile. Your object is to *unload* them. If you have a 5 of Hearts as one of your four cards, for example, and a 4 of Clubs is the top card on your 13-pile, you can move the 4 off the 13-pile and onto the 5. But if you have a 6 of Clubs on top of your 13-pile, you can't put the 5 on it. The 13-pile is *only* for unloading.

Now start turning up cards from the deck, three by three, placing them on one of the four cards, if possible, in the same pattern you used for Klondike, with each card a rank lower than the card you put it on.

As Aces appear, put them at the top of the spread—as you did in the two previous games—and build up a set in each suit, going from Ace to King.

When you open up a vacant column among the four cards in your layout, move in a card from the 13-pile to take its place.

In Canfield, as in Klondike and Russian Solitaire, the cards you play up at the top of the spread are your score.

This version is the one used for Pounce! (see page 139), but there is a more traditional way to play this game.

In the other version, before placing the four cards in front of you, put one card (the 14th) up above, where the Aces usually go. Instead of building from Aces, in this version you start building the suits from that "up" card and continue until you have built right through King and Ace and all the way back to the card that comes before it in sequence. You can't use this version so easily in Pounce! but it's fine for regular solitaire or in a two-way competition.

RUSSIAN SOLITAIRE

Some people say this is the most difficult solitaire game in the world to win.

Lay out the cards exactly as in Klondike. But instead of stopping after you finish the seven piles, lay out the rest of the deck, too, starting at the second pile—like this:

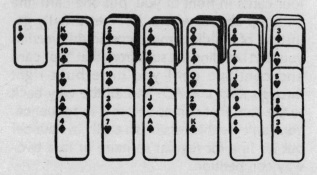

Let's follow this layout to see how the game works.

First of all, an Ace is lying exposed at

the bottom of a pile. That goes up to the top, just as in Klondike, where you will be building up Ace-to-King suits.

In the rest of the layout, you will be building *down* by suit, starting with whatever cards are available, and moving onto them the next lower card in the same suit. For example, the 6 of Diamonds is lying open. You can put the 5 of Diamonds on it—and *only* the 5 of Diamonds. Take it and put it on the 6. Your piles are uneven, but that is part of the game.

When you moved the 5 of Diamonds, you created a vacant spot in the first column that can be filled only by a King (just as in Klondike). You have a choice of which King. Suppose you decide to move in the King of Hearts. You have to move the entire column of cards on top of him to the #1 spot. There is only one card underneath the King. Turn it over: it's the King of Diamonds, and it is now the leading card in the second column.

Your next move might be to put the 4 of Diamonds on the 5 of Diamonds. That opens up the Ace of Clubs, which you can put up at the top to count as another point.

You might then move the 6 of Hearts onto the 7. Remember that when you move the 6, all the cards on top of it must move, too!

Now your layout looks like this:

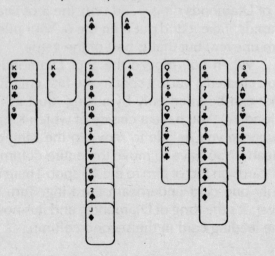

There are quite a few moves left in this game. Eventually, your layout may look like this:

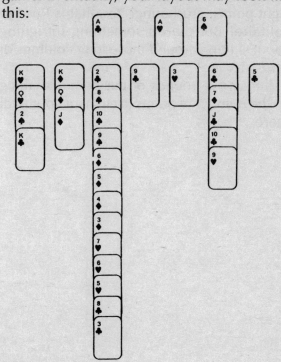

And there are more moves after that. But for all the action, you finish with a total of eight points. Frustrating? Yes, that is Russian Solitaire! But there's something intriguing about shifting around those long columns of cards. Try it.

Play five rounds of this game, totalling up the number of points in each for your total score.

THE PERSIAN CARD GAME

PLAYERS: 2

You need an ordinary deck of cards, which you divide equally between the players. The cards rank from Ace down to Two, which is low.

To start the game, the players turn the top card of their piles face up on the table, at the same time. If they turn up cards of different suits, nothing happens, and they turn up the next cards. They continue doing this until they simultaneously turn up cards of the *same suit*—such as two Diamonds, two Spades, two Hearts, or two Clubs. When that happens, the player with the *higher* card wins all the cards the other player has turned up. These go at the bottom of his or her pack.

The player who captures all the cards in the deck is the winner. Sometimes, you may go completely through the deck once or twice without turning up cards of the same suit. In that case, the game is over, and the one with the larger number of cards is the winner.

WAR

PLAYERS: 2 or 3

Never was a game more aptly named than War. It's a long—sometimes interminable—card game in which the tides of fortune swing back and forth. It requires no skill. All you need to be able to do is turn over the cards and recognize their denominations.

It starts out like the Persian Card Game and the object is the same, to capture all the cards in the deck. Divide the pack of cards in two (if three are playing, remove one card and deal 51 cards out equally).

Both players turn their top cards faceup on the table. The one who turns over the higher-ranking card wins the "trick" and takes both cards, placing them facedown at the bottom of his or her pile. The rank of cards is Ace–King–Queen–Jack–10–9–8–7–6–5–4–3–2.

When both players turn over cards of the same rank, they call, "War!" On top of their War cards, each player puts one card facedown and then another card faceup. Whoever now has the higher card on top wins all the cards in the war. If the faceup cards also match, it is "Double War!" Each player again plays a facedown card and then another faceup. The one with the higher card wins all the cards in the double war.

The player who wins all the cards in the game is the winner.

REVENGE

PLAYERS: 2

Divide the pack card by card like in War. The object of the game is to get rid of all your cards by putting them onto the other player's pack. You do it by coming up with a card that is one rank higher—or lower—than the card your opponent has just turned up.

Let's say your opponent starts the game by turning over the top card in his or her pile—and it's a 6 of Hearts. If you turn up a 7 of any suit, you can place it on your opponent's 6.

Suppose the next card you turn up is an 8. Over it goes, onto your opponent's pack, and you get another turn. Each time you get rid of a card, you get to take another turn.

You can build down, too. If the next card is another 7, you can place that on the 8 that you just put down. If the next card is not in sequence, your turn ends.

Gradually, as you play, you build up long sequences of cards, so that large numbers of cards follow each other in order. Eventually, when you get the chance to put a card on your opponent's pile, you don't put on just *one*—you put on 15 or 20 more! This is what m kes the game such fun. Your opponent can be within two cards of winning when you suddenly zap him or her with almost the whole deck—now that's revenge!

When you have gone through your pile of cards, turn them over and start again. The game goes on until one player is out of cards.

PISHE PASHA
(pronounced PISH-uh PAY-sha)

This game is played the same way as Revenge, but with one added element. Whenever an Ace comes up, it is put in the middle of the table and built on, as in Klondike. And there is no choice about putting cards up in the middle. Even if you are in the middle of a steady run of cards, you *must* interrupt it to play a card to the building suits, when it belongs there. Often, two decks are used for this game.

POUNCE!

PLAYERS: 2 to 6
EQUIPMENT: A pack of cards for each player

There is more action in this card game than in any other that has ever been invented! Actually, it isn't a game all its own, but one that has been put together.

Two or more people play their own games of solitaire—but when they put their Aces up at the top of the spread, *anyone* can build on them. It's an exciting game for three, a wild one for four, and if you have enough room (and long arms) you can even go on to six players! And then look out!

Each player needs a deck of cards, and the backs of each pack must bear a different design or emblem or color from the others, because eventually, at the end, the players sort out their own cards in order to see who won.

You can play it with any solitaire game that builds up Aces in suits, but it is most often played with Canfield or Klondike. When playing Klondike in a game of Pounce! you may run through the deck as many times as you want. Canfield makes for the fastest game.

Whichever solitaire game you choose, all the players lay out their spreads, but no one starts playing until a signal is given. Then anything goes. Play as rapidly as you can. Aces that you play to the top of the spread now go in the middle of the table. Try to get as many cards up there as rapidly as you can. These are your points. In case of a dispute, the player whose card got there first is the one who gets to leave it (that means the card that is lowest in the pile). But it is against the rules to use more than one hand to put cards in the middle. And you can play only one card up there at a time.

The first one to get rid of all the cards

onto the bases (into the middle) wins.

If play comes to a standstill before any of the players get rid of their cards, sort out the cards that have made it into the middle. The player with the most of these cards wins.

When the game is Canfield, you can play a shorter game: the one who gets rid of the 13-pile first wins. It doesn't matter where the cards go—into the middle or onto building piles—as long as they move *somewhere*.

CONCENTRATION

PLAYERS: 2 or more

Concentration is a card game which can bridge a span of generations—a four year old can play with adults or teenagers. It can also bridge the language barrier, because it is played in silence.

Lay out a deck of cards facedown any-which-way on the table. Don't let them overlap each other, and don't put them down in rows or patterns. Players take turns, and the object of the game is to turn up cards that match in number. The first player—say, Burt—turns any two cards faceup in their places. If they form a pair (two deuces, two 7's, two Kings), he removes them, puts them in his private stock, and gets another turn. If the cards do not form a pair, Burt turns them facedown again exactly as they were before. *All the players try to remember what these cards are and where they are!*

The second player—say, Maxine—turns up two cards, but now does it one at a time. If the first card is the mate to one which was previously turned up and put back, she tries to remember that card's location in order to turn up a matching card to form a pair.

Each time a player forms a pair, he or

she takes the pair into stock, gets another turn, and continues to play until two unmatched cards turn up. The game ends when all the cards have been paired off and removed. The player with the most cards in stock wins.

TIP: Sometimes your opponent's second card is the mate to a card which was turned up earlier. If you think you remember the location of both cards, but you're not sure of the earlier one, turn over the one you're not sure of first. Then, if you're wrong, you have another chance to form a matching pair.

GO FISH

PLAYERS: 2 to 5

If only two play, deal seven cards to each. If four or five play, deal five cards to each. Put the rest of the pack facedown on the table, forming the stock.

    The object of the game is to form more "books" than any other player. A book is four cards of a kind, such as four Kings, four Queens, four 7's.

The player to the dealer's left—say, Rod—begins by saying to another player: "Jane, give me your 9's. "Rod must mention the name of the player he is calling and he must say the exact rank of the card (Ace, King, Queen, for example, and he must have in hand at least one card of the rank that he calls for.

Jane must hand over all the cards she has of that rank, but if she has none, she says, "Go Fish!"

When told to "go fish," Rod must draw the top card from the stock. If it is a card of the rank he asked for, he shows the card immediately and goes again. Otherwise, the turn passes to the player on his left.

If Rod gets cards from Jane, he keeps his turn and may ask anyone for more cards. He may ask Jane again, or some different player, and he may ask for a card of any rank.

When he gets the fourth card of a book, he shows all four, places them on the table, and continues his turn. If he runs out of cards, he may draw one card from the stock at the next turn and then ask for a card of that rank. After the stock is used up and he has no cards, he is out of the game. The game ends when all 13 books have been laid down. The player with the most books wins.

AUTHORS

Since a set
of 4 cards of
the same rank
is called a book,
it's not surprising that this variation of
Go Fish is called Authors. You can play it more
seriously, though, and with greater skill.

All 52 cards are dealt out, even though
they may not come out even. When it is your
turn, you ask for a single card by naming both
its rank and suit. For example, you might say,
"Bill, give me the Jack of Spades." You continue if Bill comes up with the Jack of Spades;
otherwise, the turn passes to the person on
your left. As soon as you get a book, you show
it and put it down on the table. The game
ends when all 13 books have been laid down.

CRAZY EIGHTS

Each player is dealt seven cards. The rest of the deck goes to the middle of the table with the top card turned up beside the pack.

   The object of the game is to get rid of all the cards in your hand. Each player, in turn, places a card on the turned-up card in the middle, which matches it in rank or suit.

   Suppose the turned-up card is the Queen of Hearts. Ginny, who goes first, has a Queen of Diamonds, which matches it in rank.

Albert, who follows, has a 3 of Diamonds, which matches Ginny's card by suit. He places it on top of the Queen.

Bea, who goes next, doesn't have a 3 or a Diamond in her hand. She has to pick from the deck until she gets one, adding all those cards into her hand on one turn! She could play an 8—in the game of Crazy Eights, an 8 is wild and can be any card you want it to be. Bea may not want to play it so early in the game. On the other hand, she doesn't want to get caught with the 8 at the end of the game, as the winner will get 50 additional points.

Let's say that Bea does put down an 8. She then gets a chance to call the next suit to be played, Hearts, Spades or Clubs. She naturally wouldn't want to call Diamonds, because she doesn't have any. If she knows that one or more of the players is out of a certain suit, she can call it just to catch them.

The first one to get rid of all his or her

cards wins the round and the following points:

50 points for each 8 caught in another player's hand
10 points for each face card in another player's hand
1 point for each Ace and face value for all other cards

If the game is at a standstill because no one can put down a card and the deck is gone, then the players count up the points in their hands. The one with the lowest score is the winner, and is awarded all the points in the hands of the other players—subtracting the points in his or her own hand.

For example, Ginny has 5 points in her hand and Albert, the winner, has 3. Albert gets 2 points there. Bea has 10 points, so Albert gets them—less his own score—another 7 points. Albert's score for the round is 9.

The players go on with another round, and 100 points wins.

WILD JACKS & GO BOOM

NOTE: If you want a change from Crazy Eights, you can play Wild Jacks. Here you follow the same rules, but you use Jacks instead of 8's. Or you can play Go Boom—the same game—with no wild cards at all.

SLAP JACK

PLAYERS: 3 to 8

The object of this game, too, is to get all the cards in the deck. The only way to get the cards is to be the first one to slap a Jack when it appears in the middle of the table.

The dealer passes out the cards, one by one, until the whole deck has been dealt. The players don't look at their cards, but just make them into neat piles and start playing. Each player in turn rapidly lifts a card so that no one (including himself or herself) sees what it is until it hits the middle of the table. If the card is a Jack, the first one to slap it gets not only the Jack, but all the cards under it. That player puts all the new cards into his or her pile, and continues to play.

If anyone slaps something that turns out not to be a Jack, that player has to give one card to each player from the top of his or her pile (without looking at it first).

In case of a dispute, the lowest hand on the Jack wins.

SNIP-SNAP-SNORUM

PLAYERS: 3 or more

Here's a card game with fast action. It depends entirely on the luck of the deal, so there's no need to ponder and the game goes fast.

Deal out the entire deck so each player has the same number of cards. The first player, say, Andy, places a card faceup on the table and calls out its number, say, "Three." Now the player to the left, Michele, must either put down a 3 or say "Pass." If Michele has the matching card, she plays it on top of the first card and says "Snip."

If the next player, Steve, has a 3, he puts it down and says "Snap." The play continues around the circle until the last 3 is played. The one who puts it down says "Snorum."

The four matching cards are then pushed aside and the player who said "Snorum" puts a new card on the table, to be matched up in the same way.

If a card is played for which a player has all the matching cards, he or she plays them all and calls out, "Snip-Snap-Snorum."

You win when you get rid of all of your cards.

HEARTS

PLAYERS: 4 (2 to 6 can play, but 4 makes for the best game)

PREPARATION: If you're playing with some other number than 4, remove enough deuces from the deck to make the deal come out even.

Deal one card at a time to each player. Aces rank high. The object of the game is to avoid winning any Hearts—or to win all 13 of them.

The player at the left of the dealer makes the opening move and each of the players in turn puts one card in the middle of the table. These rounds of four cards are called "tricks." You win a trick when you play the highest card of the suit that started the round. After you win a trick, you start the next trick.

Keep score on paper. Every Heart you capture counts one point against you. The game can stop at any time, and the player with the lowest total score is the winner. If you have all 13 Hearts, you've won. Subtract 13 from your score. Some people double that score and subtract 26 points for getting all the Hearts.

CALAMITY JANE

PLAYERS: 3 to 7 (4 is the best game)

This is the most popular variation of Hearts. When most people say they want to play Hearts, they mean this game.

It is played exactly like the previous

Hearts game, with the following exceptions:

1. After the players look at their hands, they pass any three cards they choose face-down to the player at their left. Then, after they have their choice, they take into their hand the three cards that have been chosen for them by the person to the right.

2. If you capture the Queen of Spades (Calamity Jane) in one of your tricks, it counts as another point against you. Some people score Calamity Jane as 13 points against you—a real calamity—so that in one deal, you could get 25 points against you (12 points for Hearts and 13 for Calamity Jane). If you capture all 14 cards, 13 Hearts, and Calamity Jane as well, you win the round! This is called "Shooting the Moon." And if you do it, you can deduct 25 points from your score.

3. The player with the lowest score—when another player scores 50 (or 100 if you want a longer game)—wins.

LATERAL THINKING MYSTERIES

THINK TANK

THE MAN IN THE ELEVATOR

For a start, here's one of the oldest and best-known lateral thinking mysteries. It goes like this:

A man lives on the tenth floor of a building. Every day, he takes the elevator to the first floor to go to work or to go shopping. When he returns, he always takes the elevator to the seventh floor and then walks the remaining flights of stairs to his apartment on the tenth floor. Why does he do this?

Hint on page 180
Answer on page 326

BOMBS AWAY!

One night during the Second World War, an Allied bomber was on a mission over Germany. The plane was in perfect condition and everything on it worked properly. When it had reached its target, the pilot ordered the bomb doors opened. They opened. He then ordered the bombs released. They were released. But the bombs did not fall from the plane. Why should this be so?

Hint on page 181
Answer on page 326

THE COAL, CARROT, & SCARF

Five pieces of coal, a carrot, and a scarf are lying on the lawn. Nobody put them on the lawn, but there is a perfectly logical reason for their being there. What is it?

Hint on page 181
Answer on page 326

DEATH IN THE PHONE BOOTH

A man is lying dead in a telephone booth. The telephone handset is swinging. Two of the windows are broken. He was not murdered. How did he die?

Hint on page 182
Answer on page 326

THE SILENT CABBIE

A London cab driver picked up a lady who was a notorious chatterbox. He did not want to engage in conversation so he pretended to be deaf and dumb. He pointed to his mouth and ears to indicate that he could neither speak nor hear. After she alighted, he pointed to the meter so that she could see how much she owed. She paid him and then walked off. Then she realized that he could not have been a deaf mute. How did she know?

Hint on page 183
Answer on page 326

THE MEN IN THE HOTEL

Two businessmen, Mr. Smith and Mr. Jones, are booked into the same hotel for the night and given adjacent rooms on the third floor. During the night, Mr. Smith sleeps soundly. However, despite being very tired, Mr. Jones cannot fall asleep. He eventually phones Mr. Smith and falls asleep immediately after hanging up. Why should this be so?

Hint on page 184
Answer on page 327

A PECULIAR HOUSE

Mrs. Jones wanted a new house. She very much liked to see the sun shining into a room, so she instructed the builders to construct a house in which all four walls face south. After much thought, the builder managed to erect just such a house. How did he do it?

Hint on page 184
Answer on page 327

THE MAN IN THE HOUSE

A man entered a house. There was no one else in the house. He walked into a room, stopped, and then slowly raised his hands above his head. After a moment, he turned around, let out a laugh, and left. Why?

Hint on page 185
Answer on page 327

A CHESS PIECE

Two grandmasters played five games of chess. Each won the same number of games and lost the same number of games. There were no draws in any of the games. How could this be so?

Hint on pages 185-186
Answer on page 327

THE UNSEEN WALKER

On a busy Friday afternoon, a man walked several miles across London from West-minister to Knightsbridge without seeing anybody or being seen by anybody. The day was clear and bright. He had perfect eyesight and he looked where he was going. He did not travel by any method of transport other than by foot. London was thronged with people, yet not one of them saw him. How?

Hint on page 186
Answer on page 327

THE TWO SISTERS

One day, two sisters decided to clean out the old shed at the bottom of their garden. When they had finished the cleaning, one of them had a dirty face and the other had a clean face. The sister with the clean face went and washed her face, but the girl with the dirty face did not wash. Why should this be so?

Hint on page 187
Answer on page 327

THE DREAM

The boss of a storage warehouse had just arrived at work when one of his employees burst into his office. The man explained that while asleep the previous night he had dreamed that one of the stored boxes contained a bomb that would explode at two P.M., causing a terrible fire. The boss was skeptical, but agreed to investigate. After a search, a bomb was found in the area foreseen in the man's dream. The police were called, the bomb defused, and a tragedy averted. Afterwards, the boss thanked the employee sincerely and then fired him.

The sacked man had not planted the bomb, and his prophetic dream had saved the warehouse from destruction. Yet the manager was right to fire him. How could that be so?

Hint on pages 187-188
Answer on page 328

IN THE PET SHOP

A pet shop was advertising puppies for sale. Two men entered the shop. The first put ten dollars on the counter and asked for a puppy. The assistant asked whether he would prefer a poodle, a Labrador, or an Alsatian. He chose the poodle. The second man also put ten dollars on the counter and asked for a puppy. The assistant did not utter a word. He simply gave the man an Alsatian puppy. How did he know that this was what the man wanted?

Hint on pages 188–189
Answer on page 328

THE COFFEE DRINKER

A man in a restaurant complained to the waiter that there was a fly in his cup of coffee.

The waiter took the cup away and promised to bring a fresh cup of coffee. He returned a few moments later. The man tasted the coffee and complained that this was his original cup of coffee with the fly removed. He was correct, but how did he know?

Hint on page 189
Answer on page 328

HAPPY OR SAD

Three women dressed in swimsuits were standing together. Two were sad and one was happy. But the sad women were both smiling and the happy one was crying. Why should that be so?

Hint on page 190
Answer on page 328

ONE STEP BEYOND

A man stood looking through the window on the sixth floor of an office building. Suddenly, he was overcome by an impulse. He opened the window and leapt through it. It was a sheer drop outside the building to the ground. He did not use a parachute or land in water or on any special soft surface. Yet the man was completely unhurt when he landed. How could that be?

Hint on page 191
Answer on page 329

THE TURKISH BATH MYSTERY

Four men met every Thursday lunchtime at the Turkish Baths. Joe, a musician, always brought his personal cassette player so that he could listen to music. Jack, a banker, brought a thermos containing a drink. Jim and John were both lawyers and brought paperback books to read.

One day in the mist-filled room, John was found dead from a deep wound through his heart. The police were called immediately. They questioned all three suspects, but no one said they had seen anything happen. A thorough search was carried out, but no murder weapon could be found. What happened?

Hint on page 192
Answer on page 329

THE SINGLE STATEMENT

An explorer was captured by a tribe whose chief decided that the man should die. The chief was a very logical man and gave the explorer a choice. The explorer was to make a single statement. If it was true, he would be thrown over a high cliff. If it was false, he would be eaten by lions.

What statement did the clever explorer make that forced the chief to let him go?

Hint on pages 192-193
Answer on page 329

DEATH IN ROME

Mr. Jones is reading his daily newspaper. He reads an article with the following headline: "Woman Dies in Holiday Accident." It goes on to say, "Mrs. Rigby-Brown, while on holiday with her husband in Rome, fell to her death from the balcony of her seventh-floor room."

Mr. Jones turns to his wife and says, "That was not an accident. It was murder." He had never met either of the Rigby-Browns, so how could he know it was murder?

Hint on page 194
Answer on page 329

HINTS
for Lateral Thinking Mysteries

The Man in the Elevator

Q: Is there anything that he does between the seventh and tenth floors other than climb stairs?

A: No.

Q: If he had someone else with him, would they both get out at the seventh floor and walk up to the tenth floor?

A: No.

Q: If he lived on the sixth floor, would he go up to the sixth floor in the elevator?

A: Yes.

Q: If he lived in a different block of apartments in a different country but still on the 10th floor, would he still get out on the 7th floor when going up?

A: Most probably yes.

Bombs Away!

Q: Would the fact that the bomb did not fall surprise any of the crew?

A: No.

Q: If that same plane were parked on the runway and the bomb doors were opened and the bombs released, would they fall?

A: Yes.

Q: Was the way in which the plane was flying the cause of the bombs not dropping?

A: Yes.

The Coal, Carrot, and Scarf

Q: Does the time of year matter?

A: Yes.

Q: Were the coal, carrot, and scarf brought out to the garden by human beings?

A: Yes.

Q: Were they used for some entertainment purpose?

A: Yes.

HINTS
for Lateral Thinking Mysteries
(continued)

182

Death in the Phone Booth

Q: Was he talking to someone when he died?

A: Yes.

Q: Was his death an accident?

A: No.

Q: Did anything external hit the phone booth?

A: No.

Q: Did he break the phone booth windows?

A: Yes.

Clue: There was a fishing rod outside the phone booth.

The Silent Cabbie

This little problem is best solved by thinking clearly about how a passenger uses a taxi. What communications take place between passenger and cabbie?

HINTS
for Lateral Thinking Mysteries
(continued)

The Men in the Hotel

Q: Was there something happening in Mr. Smith's room that was preventing Mr. Jones from sleeping?

A: Yes.

Q: Was it a noise?

A: Yes.

Q: Did they speak for long on the phone?

A: No.

A Peculiar House

This house had only four walls and they all faced south. Think about the shape of the house, then think about where it might be located.

The Man in the House

Q: Was he frightened when he raised his hands?

A: Yes.

Q: Was it his house?

A: No.

Q: Had he heard a sound that made him raise his hands?

A: Yes.

Q: Did he laugh because he was surprised and relieved?

A: Yes.

A Chess Piece

This is a kind of problem that depends on the reader or listener making the wrong initial assumptions. Test all the assumptions with questions like the following:

Q: Were they playing normal chess?

A: Yes.

Q: In chess, if one player wins then the other loses?

A: Yes, always.

Q: So when one grandmaster won a game, the other grandmaster lost it?

A: No.

Q: Was there anybody else involved?

A: Yes.

The Unseen Walker

Q: If he walked into this room now, would we see him and he see us?

A: Yes.

Q: Did he wear anything special?

A: Yes. Clue: It was a miner's helmet.

Q: Did he walk along normal roads?

A: No.

The Two Sisters

This is another problem that involves making the wrong assumptions. In this case, you need to question the assumptions and motivations of the two girls.

Q: Did the girl who washed want to clean her face?

A: Yes.

Q: Did she think her face was dirty?

A: Yes.

Q: So the girl who did not wash thought that her face was already clean?

A: Yes.

The Dream

Q: Was the man sacked because he had had anything to do with planting the bomb?

A: No.

Q: Had the man genuinely dreamed about the bomb?

A: Yes.

Q: Did the boss have a grudge of some kind against the man?

A: No.

Q: Were the man's particular responsibilities relevant?

A: Yes.

In the Pet Shop

Q: Was this the last puppy?

A: No, there were plenty of all three breeds.

Q: Were any of the three men known to each other?

A: No.

Q: Did the second man gesture in any way that he wanted the Alsatian?

A: No.

Q: Had the customer ever been in the shop before?

A: No.

Clue: Every dog has his price.

The Coffee Drinker

Q: Was there something about the cup itself that identified it?

A: No.

Q: Was the fly still in the cup?

A: No.

Q: Could the man have known that it was the same cup if he had not tasted it?

A: No.

HINTS
for Lateral Thinking Mysteries
(continued)

Happy or Sad
Q: Were they on the beach or at a swimming pool?
A: No.
Q: Were they beautiful, shapely women?
A: Yes.
Q: Was the happy one crying because she was happy?
A: Yes.
Q: Were the sad ones smiling because they were sad?
A: No.

One Step Beyond
Q: Was he holding a rope?
A: No.

Q: Did he have special powers or could any-one have done this?

A: Anyone could have done this.

Q: Did he fall from six floors and land on the ground outside the building?

A: No.

Q: Did he jump through the window?

A: Yes.

HINTS
for Lateral Thinking Mysteries
(continued)

The Turkish Bath Mystery

Q: Was John murdered by one of his three companions?

A: Yes.

Q: Did the murderer bring the weapon into the baths with him?

A: Yes.

Q: Could the police have found the weapon if they had searched harder?

A: No.

The Single Statement

The explorer must make a statement that is both true and false at the same time. Better still, it should be a statement that means that any action the chief takes would place him in the position of having acted illogically.

Can you construct a statement about the way the explorer will die that is neither true nor false?

Death in Rome

Q: Had Mr. Jones ever met either of the Rigby-Browns?

A: No.

Q: Was he right in saying it was murder?

A: Yes.

Q: Was Mr. Rigby-Brown the murderer?

A: Yes.

Q: Had Mr. Jones ever communicated in any way with Mrs. Rigby-Brown?

A: No.

Q: Had Mr. Jones, in his professional capacity, provided some service to Mr. Rigby-Brown?

A: Yes.

Q: Did he deduce from this service and the newspaper article that Mrs. Rigby-Brown had been murdered?

A: Yes.

WORD SEARCH PUZZLES

The Simpsons

```
D L E I F G N I R P S
T O D H E O S P A A R
Y E N R A B B C P E E
B A A U L I E M N S N
W A K H T O A S I E N
H M R B U R N S D J I
Y O A T G W U F N P K
H O B N O M L C E C S
C A A S K A I I L A R
T O P N N R G A S R U
A R P D E G U I O K O
R A E N A E L S N T M
C R L M G Y H C T I Y
S A N D O K O O D Y E
O S S R E H T I M S S
```

Answer on page 330

BARNEY	MAGGIE
BART	MARGE
DONUT	MR. BURNS
EDNA KRABAPPEL	NED FLANDERS
GRAMPA	NELSON
HOMER	OTTO
ITCHY	SCRATCHY
JIMBO	SEYMOUR SKINNER
KRUSTY	SMITHERS
LISA	SPRINGFIELD

Circling the Bases

```
            B T C
          A E H E A
        S T R I K E T
        E E Y I E V R U C
      H O I U P N R E M O H
      I G E R S M T M T A C J E
    T T R O E P U R E T T A B K R
    P N R E S O U T F I E L D L B
    L U O N D E C K P H E A G A U
      B E E L I R D F O U L C B
        W K R A L S E N A K G
          E O I F S R I S F
          W H T E R T E
            H C A O C
              N P R
```

Answer on page 331

BACKSTOP	FOUL
BALK	HOMER
BASE HIT	NO-HITTER
"BATTER UP!"	ON DECK
BUNT	OUTFIELD
CATCHER	SLIDER
CHOKE UP	STRIKE
COACH	UMPIRE
CURVE	WILD PITCH
ERROR	WORLD SERIES

Monopoly Game

```
E  T  N  E  R  M  Y  P  O  N  B
O  S  K  R  O  W  R  E  T  A  W
S  E  U  P  O  O  L  Y  N  P  R
O  H  P  O  P  E  R  K  T  O  I
E  C  O  E  H  N  E  K  O  T  M
S  Y  R  R  O  R  A  R  E  N  K
L  T  X  A  T  Y  R  U  X  U  L
Y  I  A  M  E  L  A  E  D  D  A
A  N  A  F  L  T  I  E  I  R  W
S  U  T  J  R  C  L  N  C  E  D
E  M  T  S  H  I  R  N  E  A  R
R  M  T  A  L  A  O  M  N  T  A
D  O  N  O  T  P  A  S  S  G  O
I  C  L  C  C  G  D  I  T  Y  B
E  C  A  L  P  K  R  A  P  N  J
```

Answer on page 331

BANKER	LUXURY TAX
BOARDWALK	MONEY
CHANCE	PARK PLACE
COMMUNITY CHEST	PROPERTY
DICE	RAILROAD
DO NOT PASS GO	RENT
GAME	ROLL
HOTEL	SHORT LINE
HOUSE	TOKEN
JAIL	WATER WORKS

Piece a Pizza

```
N O O O M A E F T
 T T A N C H O V I E S
 T E L A R A H O I W I T Y
O S U G A S L M I L N C E A
B U E M U S H R O O M I
R R T R Y E O U R R
O C L H E G A E
C I L R A G P
C V A E T P R O
O O B A E L D U M I
L S T P T A T H B I S P
I W A A A N P A R M E S A N
 S E U M T S A U S A G E E
 M A C O S Y T A S H P
 I E E T O N I O N
```

Answer on page 332

ANCHOVIES	ONION
BROCCOLI	OREGANO
CRUST	PARMESAN
EGGPLANT	PEPPERONI
FETA	PESTO
GARLIC	ROMANO
HAMBURGER	SALT
MEATBALL	SAUCE
MUSHROOM	SAUSAGE
OLIVE	TOMATO

By the Numbers

```
E  C  A  R  D  E  G  G  E  L  3
T  H  2  E  E  E  3  2  S  P  2
3  D  5  O  T  9  I  T  E  O  1
2  W  O  H  G  F  4  A  B  E  S
S  S  A  S  B  C  T  S  A  A  A
E  L  L  Y  E  D  E  9  B  1  Y
S  1  S  M  B  V  4  E  Y  E  S
S  E  T  E  I  U  C  O  L  B  A
A  U  Y  L  1  A  L  W  O  A  E
L  Y  9  K  T  T  I  B  N  C  C
G  4  H  C  L  U  B  K  5  O  E
D  T  H  U  2  S  O  1  L  N  A
3  2  1  B  L  A  S  T  O  F  F
2  B  Y  2  O  E  4  I  N  N  G
7  4  4  1  7  5  E  K  A  T  1
```

Answer on page 332

BABYLON 5

CATCH-22

COLT .45

EASY AS 1, 2, 3

49ER

4-EYES

4-H CLUB

9 LIVES

9 TO 5

1-ON-1

1, 2, BUCKLE MY SHOE

R2-D2

TAKE 5

3-D GLASSES

3-LEGGED RACE

3-PEAT

3-2-1 BLASTOFF!

3-WAY BULB

2-BY-4

2 IF BY SEA

Modern Electronics

```
H  C  T  A  W  S  C  H  V  O  X
W  M  V  R  T  A  R  A  T  O  S
N  Y  C  E  E  E  I  T  B  E  A
E  M  R  S  T  M  H  M  E  L  T
N  E  S  N  E  C  O  R  W  E  E
O  O  I  D  A  O  I  T  R  D  L
H  R  I  Y  M  B  O  D  E  M  L
P  O  U  T  R  P  K  P  N  P  I
L  A  A  R  A  U  A  L  N  E  T
L  N  G  T  S  T  H  A  A  V  E
E  E  A  E  O  E  S  T  C  W  D
C  Y  O  E  R  R  U  Y  S  R  I
O  I  D  A  R  M  F  M  A  A  S
N  I  N  T  E  N  D  O  G  L  H
V  O  I  C  E  M  A  I  L  E  P
```

Answer on page 333

AM-FM RADIO	REMOTE
BOOMBOX	SATELLITE DISH
CABLE	SCANNER
CELL PHONE	STEREO
COMPUTER	SWATCH
MODEM	VCRS
NINTENDO	VIDEOTAPE
PAGER	VOICE MAIL
PLAYSTATION	WALKMAN
PRINTER	WEB TV

Feeling Lucky?

```
K N O C K O N W O O D
C F L L A B T H G I E
A I N D E M S I C S N
R T H I R T E E N U G
C A C A B K H E V P N
A A H D G S A U P E P
N C A E I N N E M R N
O Y N W B I S O R S T
P H C J I N X R O T U
E O E C G S A H T I S
T T G O U I H L B T R
S I N N N R O B G I G
R A B B I T S F O O T
O O O D T B L E U N C
K W H O R S E S H O E
```

Answer on page 333

BIG BREAK	LOTTO
BINGO	OMEN
CHANCE	RABBIT'S FOOT
CHARM	RAINBOW
CURSE	SEVEN
DICE	STEP ON A CRACK
EIGHT BALL	STREAK
HORSESHOE	SUPERSTITION
JINX	THIRTEEN
KNOCK ON WOOD	WISHBONE

"Oh, Horrors!"

```
D R O T A N I M R E T
M E O R I E L U O H G
H O M L S R R M O R M
O V B O G E Y M A N M
I O O E N S K Y H I O
G O D Z I L L A A E N
V E Y H A D L C N T S
M O S U S N T I T S T
E D N R N A S C V N E
G R A V E R O B B E R
A H T U I R H L A K D
L T C H L A G N A N N
O Y H T A O T O E A H
N E E R I H T I A R W
M O R N S W F T E F R
```

Answer on page 334

ALIENS	GODZILLA
BODY SNATCHER	GRAVE ROBBER
BOGEYMAN	MEGALON
DEMON	MONSTER
DEVIL	MUMMY
FIEND	OGRE
FRANKENSTEIN	SNAKES
GHOST	TERMINATOR
GHOUL	WITCH
GOBLIN	WRATH

Famous Last Words

```
B R T I L L S C N T A
R E V L I S O Y I H E
X G G A T T I I O A C
M N T O B E D L S T O
A A A Y O U A O N S M
T R A R S D G A I A E
M T R C O S H O O L B
F S R I U A T O F L A
T A A H V Y O L E F C
M E R A C E K A T O K
R B E E L E D T H L A
S T T D W S A E L K A
V N O I S E T R R S A
U O Y E V O L I B C A
T D B Y G N O L O S I
```

Answer on page 334

"ADIOS"   "I LOVE YOU"
"ALOHA"   "LATER"
"ARRIVEDERCI"   "SCRAM!"
"BE GOOD"   "SEE YA"
"BUG OFF!"   "SHOO!"
"CIAO"   "SO LONG"
"COME BACK!"   "TAKE CARE"
"DON'T BE A STRANGER"   "TA-TA"
"FAREWELL"   "THAT'S ALL, FOLKS!"
"HI-YO, SILVER!"   "TOODLE-OO!"

SHERLOCK HOLMES MYSTERIES

HAPPY BIRTHDAY, DEAR SHERLOCK

Sherlock Holmes and Dr. Watson were relaxing by the fire in the study of 221b Baker Street. Holmes was puffing on his favorite pipe while Watson was reading the *Times*. Suddenly, Watson glanced over the top of the newspaper and looked directly at Holmes. "When is your birthday, Holmes?" he asked.

"You tell me, Watson," Holmes replied with a smile. "The day before yesterday I was thirty two, and next year I will be thirty five!"

"Impossible!" snapped Watson.

But Holmes was right. Can you tell on what day of the year Holmes celebrated his birthday?

Answer on page 335

WISHING WELL

While working on a case Dr. Watson accidentally fell down a 30–foot dry wishing well. Sherlock Holmes lowered him down a rope.

"Can you climb up?" shouted Holmes.

"I'll be out before you know it!" came Watson's reply.

But the climb wasn't as easy as Watson had first imagined. Each hour he managed to climb 3 feet—but slipped back 2 feet.

How long did it take Watson to get out?

Answer on page 335

WISHING
WELL

ORDER OF FINISH

Holmes and Watson decided to have a quiet day at the races. They arrived in time to catch the first race. The race was between five horses: MANOR PARK, PEANUTS, ROYAL MILE, DUSKY and EASTERN CLASSIC.

MANOR PARK finished in front of PEANUTS, but behind ROYAL MILE. DUSKY finished in front of EASTERN CLASSIC, but behind PEANUTS.

In which order did they finish the race?

Answer on page 335

THREE THIEVES

Sherlock Holmes apprehended three thieves; Robert, Walter, and Frank. Each of them had robbed a house in a different part of London at approximately the same time. Robert, who was the oldest, didn't commit his crime in Ealing, and Walter didn't rob the house in Clapham. The one who robbed the house in Ealing didn't steal the gold watch. The one who robbed the house in Clapham stole the landscape painting. Walter didn't steal the silver coins.

In what part of London did Frank commit his crime and what did he steal?

Answer on page 335

MESSAGE
FROM MORIARTY

Holmes received a hand–delivered note that he studied for a short time before passing to Watson.

"It's some sort of code!" exclaimed Watson. "What does it mean and who is it from?"

Holmes grabbed his hat and coat. "It's from Moriarty, Watson. Hurry, we must stop him!"

The message read:

> J XJMM SPC UIF CBOL PG
> FOHMBOE UPOJHIU.
> NPSJBSUZ.

Holmes had obviously deciphered the message. Can you?

Answer on page 335

SNOOKER

Holmes and Watson were having a relaxing game of snooker in their club when they were joined by Inspector Lestrade and his sergeant. Someone suggested that they have a competition using only the fifteen red balls. For each red ball sunk the player would receive one point. The four of them would play each other once. Each game would end when all the red balls had been sunk. The winner of the competition would be the player who scored the most points.

1. Holmes scored twice as many points as Watson in their game.
2. Only one point separated Holmes and Lestrade in their game.
3. Watson beat the sergeant by five points.
4. The sergeant scored one less point against Holmes than he did against Watson.

5. Watson sank seven balls more than Lestrade.
6. Holmes finished with an odd number of points.
7. The sergeant finished with eighteen points.

Who won the competition and how many points did each player score?

Answer on page 336

COUNTRY DINNER

General Smithers invited five people to his country house for dinner. The surnames of the guests were: Forest, Giles, Handy, Jackson and King. Their vocations were: doctor, actress, lawyer, banker and writer (but not necessarily in that order). During the meal Smithers dropped dead from food poisoning. The poison had been slipped into his meal by one of the guests. When Sherlock Holmes arrived on the scene he was given the following information:

1. Jackson arrived last, the doctor arriving just ahead of her.
2. The writer and the actress arrived before Giles.
3. Third to arrive was the lawyer, just ahead of King.

4. Forest had seen the actress put the poison on Smither's plate.

Holmes took the actress to Scotland Yard for further questioning. Who was the actress?

Answer on page 336

THE SAFETY DEPOSIT BOX

While working on a case Holmes received vital information from a mysterious source in the form of a note.

The note read:

"Go to the Dunwick Bank. Inside each of the safety deposit boxes listed below you will find a clue to the crime you are presently investigating.

"BOX NUMBERS: 20, 80, 76, 19, 23, 92, 88, and ?

"I have omitted to tell you the number of the last box, but I'm sure a great detective such as yourself will know where to look."

Holmes read the note then passed it to Dr. Watson.

"Most inconvenient," muttered Watson. "Now we'll have to open every single safety deposit box to find the clue."

"Not so, Watson," replied Holmes. "I know exactly which box to open. Come along, let's hurry to the Dunwick Bank."

What was the number of the last safety deposit box?

Answer on page 336

VICTIM MEETING

Eight men, all of whom had recently been robbed by Professor Moriarty, met in a conference room of a fashionable London Hotel. Sherlock Holmes had received an invitation to attend the meeting. When Holmes arrived he found the eight men sitting at a table (see diagram below). From the following information can you identify the position of each man at the table and his vocation?

```
     (2)          (3)          (4)
(1) [                              ] (5)
     (8)          (7)          (6)
```

1. The Vet and the Dentist sat opposite each other.

2. The chairman of the meeting sat in position one, with Adams to his left.

230

3. Wilson sat in an even–numbered position with the Banker to his left.

4. The Doctor had the Solicitor to his right.

5. Clark, not Brown, sat in position three, directly opposite the Butcher.

6. The Baker sat in position five, with Jones to his left and Dawson to his right.

7. Smith sat to the left of the Vet.

8. Black, who sat opposite Clark, had the Surgeon on his left.

Answer on page 336

MORE FROM MORIARTY

"I've just received a note from Moriarty," Holmes informed Dr. Watson. "He intends to rob a house on Baker Street this evening."

"Great Scot, which house, Holmes?" inquired Watson.

"That's just it, Watson. He doesn't say, but he has given us several clues."

From the clues listed below can you work out the number of the house Moriarty intends to rob?

1. The last digit is twice the first digit.
2. The sum of the first digit and the last digit is equal to the second digit.
3. The sum of all three digits is twice that of the second digit.

Answer on page 336

258

233

SYNCHRONIZE YOUR WATCHES!

Holmes and Watson had set their pocket watches to the same time. Unknown to them, Watson's watch was running exactly two minutes per hour slow, and the watch belonging to Holmes was going exactly a minute per hour too fast. Later, when they checked their watches again, it was discovered that the watch belonging to Holmes was exactly one hour ahead of Watson's watch.

How long had it been since they had originally set their watches?

Answer on page 337

WHO'S WHO AT THE TABLE?

Holmes had been introduced to four musicians: two men, Frank and Harold, and two women, Ethel and Georgina.

One played the french horn, another the cymbals, the third was a trumpeter and the fourth, like Holmes, a violinist. All four were seated at a square table.

From the clues listed below can you identify the musician who played the same instrument as Holmes?

1. The person who sat across from Frank played the french horn.
2. The person who sat across from Harold was not the trumpeter.
3. The person who sat on Ethel's left played the cymbals.

4. The person on Georgina's left was not the violinist.
5. The trumpeter and the violinist were brother and sister.

Answer on page 337

LIBRARY BOOKS

Holmes, Watson, Lestrade, Moriarty and Mrs. Hudson all belonged to the same library. All five were returning books at the same time. The library shelved its books in alphabetical order by title instead of author.

Borrower	**Title**
Holmes	GREAT DETECTIVES
Watson	MEDICINE
Hudson	THE COOK BOOK
Moriarty	GREAT CRIMINALS
Lestrade	POLICE

1. None of the borrowers returned the book listed against their name above.
2. Two books were overdue. Watson had one, the other was "MEDICINE."
3. The books returned by Holmes and Watson sat next to each other on the shelf.

4. Mrs. Hudson had to pay a fine for a late return.

Can you match up all five titles with the borrowers?

Answer on page 337

THE CASE OF THE HARD-BOILED EGG

As part of his own specially devised diet, Dr. Watson needed to eat, every day, an egg that had been boiled for 15 minutes. On the first day he asked Mrs. Hudson to prepare the egg for him.

"I only have a 7-minute hourglass and an 11-minute hourglass," complained Mrs. Hudson. "So it can't be done."

"Of course it can," interrupted Holmes, and he proceeded to show Mrs. Hudson how.

Can you find the QUICKEST way to time the boiling of the egg?

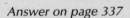

Answer on page 337

241

LUCKY PENNY

Stand with your back to the wall with your head and heels touching it. Try to pick up a penny without moving your heels. If you can get it, you're very lucky!

A TOUCHY PROBLEM

Try this: pat your head gently with one hand in an up-and-down motion. At the same time rub your stomach in a circular motion with the other hand.

Now reverse the motions: Pat your head and rub your stomach, whistle, rub your head and pat your stomach, whistle, and so on. Most people get the two movements hopelessly confused.

PAT & RUB

1. Make a circle with your left foot while you make a figure 6 in the air with your left arm.

> Switch the direction
> of your foot circle.

> Now do it with your
> right arm and foot.

> Now use your left arm
> and your right foot.

2. Make a circle with your left foot while you make a figure 8 in the air with your left arm.

> Switch the direction
> of your foot circle.

> Now do it with your
> right arm and foot.

> Now use your left arm
> and your right foot.

STUCK TO THE WALL

Stand with your head, shoulder, one side and its heel tight against the wall. Now try to move the outside leg without moving any other part of your body away from the wall.

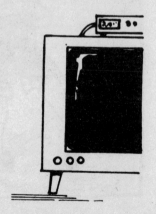

THE RUBBER THUMB

#1 #2

Hold one thumb straight up and grasp it tightly with your other hand (see Illustration 1). Illustration 2 shows how this trick appears from the front. The thumb of the top hand is shoved under the index finger of that hand. When the end peeks out, it looks as if it is the end of the thumb on your lower hand.

First get into the position in Illustration 1. Start "pulling" on that *lower* thumb and make faces as if you are in great pain. Actually, you're not pulling at all. You are just moving your upper hand slowly up the thumb that is being "stretched." Wiggle your lower hand back and forth with great effort, and slowly slip the end of your thumb under your index finger so it peeks out at the top.

"Stretch" your thumb as far as you can without giving yourself away. As soon as the end of your lower thumb starts to appear, slide your upper hand all the way back down to the lower hand with a sudden jerk—as if the stretched thumb were snapping back into place. Then open your hand quickly and begin massaging the "rubber" thumb as though you can still feel the pain.

Younger spectators will be especially pleased by this trick and will watch—fascinated—as you torture your thumb.

Practice the trick in front of a mirror until you get the impression yourself that your thumb is being stretched. If you can't fool yourself, who can you fool?

THE IRRESISTIBLE FORCE

Bend your fingers and put your hands together, so that your fingers meet at the second joint, as in the illustration.

Now move out your third fingers (the tall ones) on each hand, so that they are pointing up and leaning against each other. Get your fingers tightly joined again at the second joint.

Now try to separate your third fingers without separating your other fingers.

THE BROKEN FINGER

If you are tricky enough with your fingers, not only can you stretch your thumb, but you can even seem to break off your index finger.

#1

First, hold your hands as shown in Illustration 1. Then place your bent thumb right up against your index finger, which you have also bent. Now you need to cover up the spot where your thumb and index finger touch. Do this simply by placing the index finger of your upper hand over that place (see Illustration 2). This makes it look like a whole finger, even though it is just the combination

of one thumb joint with one index finger
joint.

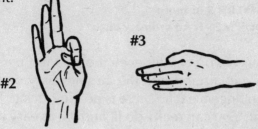

#3

#2

Now quickly slide the hand with the
thumb-part away, without changing the
position of any of your fingers (see Illustration
3). Your audience will think that your finger
has actually broken off!

Before they can recover from their
shock, slide your hands back together. The
"broken" finger is together again! Then
stretch out your finger normally and rub the
"wound." Your puzzled spectators will try to
figure out how you did it—so that they can do
it themselves.

LIFT A FRIEND

PLAYERS: 5 or more
EQUIPMENT: An ordinary chair

Four of you can lift even the heaviest person off a chair and into the air with only one or two fingers each. There is no gimmick to this feat. You can really do it, and it's as easy as it looks!

Let one of the group sit in the chair. Then the four of you who will do the lifting stand at the four corners of the chair. At a signal, you each take a deep breath and hold it. Then two of you put one or two fingers under the knees of the person in the chair, and the other two players put their fingers under the person's arms. Still holding your breath, you lift the person out of the chair and up into the air as if he or she weighed almost nothing at all!

It is holding your breath that is the key to this feat. Don't let your breath go until the person is back in the chair.

KEEP FROM LAUGHING

PLAYERS: 6 or more
EQUIPMENT: A handkerchief

The players form a circle. One of them stands in the middle, throws a handkerchief up in the air, and starts laughing. Everyone in the circle laughs too, until the handkerchief hits the floor. At that moment there is complete silence. Anyone who laughs is out.

THINK FAST

PLAYERS: 3 or more
EQUIPMENT: None

The players sit in a circle and they set up a rhythm by tapping their thighs twice, clapping hands twice in front of them, and snapping their fingers twice at about shoulder level —in that order. The first player begins by saying "Category" on one set of finger snaps, and then giving the name of the category on the next set of snaps. The category should be a broad one, such as trees, fruits, or flowers, television shows, desserts, or breeds of dogs.

All the players keep up the tap-tap, clap-clap, snap-snap rhythm straight through as the player to the left names something in the category on the next snap, ending the name by the second snap. The next player to the left must give another name on the next snap, and so on until somebody misses—like this:

#1 (tap-tap, clap-clap) **Category** (as they snap).
   (tap-tap, clap-clap) **Countries** (as they snap).
#2 (tap-tap, clap-clap) **England** (as they snap).
#3 (tap-tap, clap-clap) **Fiji** (as they snap).
#4 (tap-tap, clap-clap) **United States** (as they snap).
#5 (tap-tap, clap-clap) **Er**—(as they snap).

Player #5 is out. Player #6 starts the whole process again, naming a new category. Play until there is only one person left, the winner.

Easy? There's one more requirement. You can't repeat a name. Wait till you're all set to say your word and the player before you says it! You have about three seconds to come up with another name that hasn't been said before. Remember, the name of the object must be given in rhythm. And if your tongue gets tangled up, that's a miss, too!

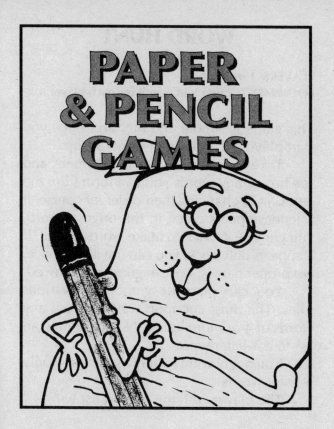

PAPER & PENCIL GAMES

WORD HUNT

PLAYERS: 1 or more
EQUIPMENT: Paper and pencil for each player

This game is simple and fun, and once you start playing it, you don't want to stop.

Take a word of about 8 or 10 letters, and see how many words you can form from the letters in it, changing their order, of course. If a letter appears twice in the original word, you can use it twice to make words with it. If it appears only once, you can use it only once. No proper names, no foreign words allowed.

You can play the game with various rules. The most common way is to use any words of 4 or more letters. No fair adding an "s" to a 3-letter word.

You might want to play by allowing only 5-letter words.

The player with the longest list wins.

Hint: It is easier to keep track of your words and not duplicate them if you set up your page by numbering down in the left-hand margin, and then starting each column of words with a different letter (see below):

HAPPINESS

1	happen	apse	pine	sane	nape
2	hasp	aspen	pane	sine	
3	hiss	ashen	pass	spine	
4			pain	shine	
5				snip	
6				snap	
7				spin	
8				shin	
9				ship	
10				shape	
11				snipe	

Here are some words to start with. If you want to test yourself against this book, you'll find lists of 4–and–more–letter words starting on page 338. Allow yourself 10 minutes for each hunt, 1 point for each word.

AMELIORATE		IRREGULARLY	
Poor	0–25	Poor	0–15
Fair	26–50	Fair	16–25
Good	51–80	Good	26–35
Very Good	81–100	Very Good	36–45
Excellent	over 100	Excellent	over 45

PRECIOUS		DEVELOPING	
Poor	0–15	Poor	0–20
Fair	16–25	Fair	21–30
Good	26–35	Good	31–40
Very Good	36–45	Very Good	41–60
Excellent	over 45	Excellent	over 60

CONSTRUCTION		ESTABLISH	
Poor	0–20	Poor	0–20
Fair	21–30	Fair	21–30
Good	31–45	Good	31–40
Very Good	46–60	Very Good	41–60
Excellent	over 60	Excellent	over 60

Answers on pages 338–341

LONGEST WORD

PLAYERS: 2 or more
EQUIPMENT: Paper and pencil for each player

You start this game with a one-letter word (A or I) and add letters one at a time. Each time you add a new letter it must form another word, and at no time can you change the order of the previous letters. But you may add the new letter at the beginning or the end, or insert it anywhere inside the word. The object is to see who can form the longest word. Following is a sample game:

A
AY
SAY
STRAY
ASTRAY
ASHTRAY
ASHTRAYS

DOTS

PLAYERS: 2
EQUIPMENT: Pencil and paper

Take a large sheet of paper and make as many
rows of dots as you want. Then each player
takes a turn and draws a line connecting one
dot with the next in any direction—except
diagonally—and in any part of the diagram.

Try to connect the dots so that they make
little squares. The one to draw the line that
finishes a square initials the closed square
and then is required to draw an extra line. The
player with the most initialed squares wins.

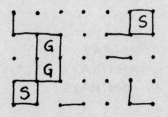

ETERNAL TRIANGLES

PLAYERS: 2
EQUIPMENT: Pencil and paper

This game is similar to Dots. Cover a sheet of
paper with dots starting with one in the first
row, 2 in the second, 3 in the third, and so on
as far as you care to go, as in the diagram
here.

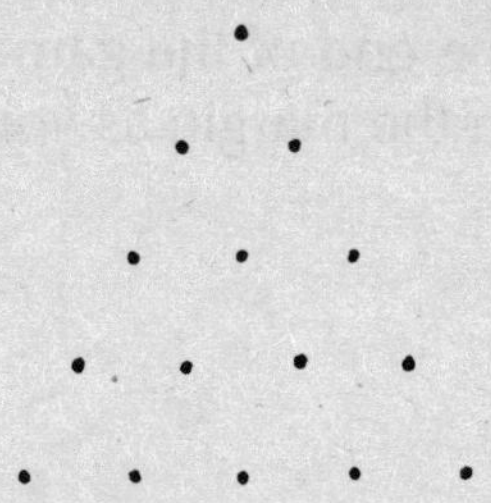

```
            •

          •

        •   •   •

      •   •   •   •

    •   •   •   •   •
```

Each player in turn draws a line
connecting two of the dots either horizontally
or diagonally, and the object is to form an

enclosed triangle. The player who adds the line which forms the enclosed triangle, initials it and goes again until he or she fails to form a triangle.

The player who makes the most triangles wins.

You can make this game more difficult if you score extra points for large triangles made at a turn. If you use colored pencils to mark off the larger triangles, you can score them up at the end of the game, or you can score them in the margin as you go along.

SNAKES

PLAYERS: 2 to 4
EQUIPMENT: Pencil and paper

Here is another relative of Dots.

Setup a bunch of dots on your paper, the same as for the previous games. Now, starting anywhere you like, take turns drawing lines from dot to dot, but don't make boxes. Instead, make a long, stiff snake. No diagonal lines allowed. No skipping spaces.

The winner is the last one to be able to draw a line without connecting the snake to itself.

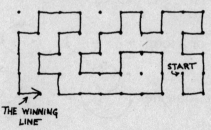

THE WINNING LINE

START

SPROUTS

PLAYERS: 2
EQUIPMENT: Paper and pencil for each player

In this game you start with just three or four dots on a piece of paper, and join them together. But it's not like the other games because here the line doesn't have to be straight. It can be straight if you want, but it's more interesting when it "sprouts" in

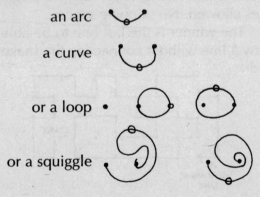

an arc

a curve

or a loop

or a squiggle

For example, start with good solid dots—in fact, let's call them blops. Then take turns joining one blop to another and, after you finish, put a new blop somewhere on the line.

What's the catch? You may not cross a line

and no blop may have more than 3 sprouts coming out of it. As soon as you attach your third sprout to the blop, put a slash through it

(it makes it easier to see) so that you know that blop is out of play. When you get expert, maybe you'll decide to leave the slashes out.

The winner is the one who makes the last possible move.

Here is a game you might play:

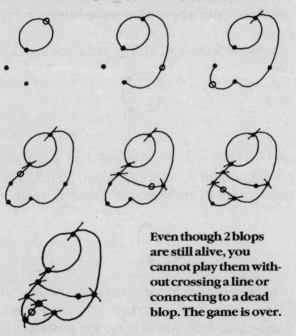

Even though 2 blops are still alive, you cannot play them without crossing a line or connecting to a dead blop. The game is over.

DICTIONARY

PLAYERS: 4 to 8
EQUIPMENT: An unabridged dictionary
          Paper and pencil for scorekeeping

One player is "It" and looks through the dictionary for a word whose meaning is likely to be unknown to the other players.

Let's say that Keith selects the word "paronymous." He goes on to give a definition of it to the other players. However, he must define it in his own words—not just read it from the dictionary—and the definition he gives them does not necessarily have to be right.

Keith might say that "paronymous" means "similar to," for example, and add that it comes from the root "para," which means "related to." Keith made that up.

The other players have to decide whether or not they believe that Keith has given them a correct definition of the word. Keith gets one point for every player who guesses wrong.

The player to Keith's right goes next.

Note: "Paronymous" is an adjective that refers to words "containing the same root or stem." "Lively" and "life" are "paronymous" words.

GAMES OF SKILL OR STRENGTH

TABLE FOOTBALL

PLAYERS: 2 (more can play in round-robin
       tournaments)

EQUIPMENT: A sheet of paper
       Table (ideal length for beginners is at least
       40 inches or 1 meter, but you can play on
       a table of any length)
       Any flat surface, such as a book or ruler

PREPARATION: Using the sheet of paper, make
       the football as follows:

1.

2.

3.

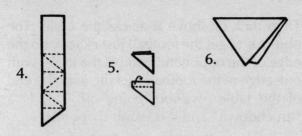

4.　　　5.　　　6.

Flip a coin to see who goes first.

THE FIRST MOVE: Set the football on end at the edge of the table as in Illustration 7.

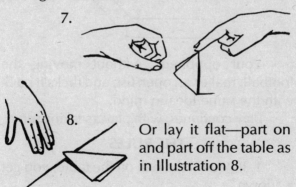

7.

8.

Or lay it flat—part on and part off the table as in Illustration 8.

273

Then flick or shove it across the table. The object is to get the football just exactly on the edge of the opponent's side of the table, with one edge of the football sticking over the end of the table—*without going off.* This is a "touchdown" and it is worth six points.

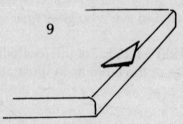

Your opponent, without moving the football, makes an open fist, and flicks it back with the same idea in mind.

Play continues, with players taking turns.

THE RULES

1. If you hit the ball off the table, you get a "down."

It is up to your opponent then, to put the ball back in play, starting as in Illustration 7 or 8, from his or her end of the table.

2. When you have made four downs of your own, your opponent gets a chance for a field goal. (See Rule 6.)

3. Touchdown: When you get a touchdown, it is worth six points and a try at an extra point. This "try" is a chance to make a field goal. (See Rule 6.)

4. You may not hit the football with your thumb or cover the football with your hand at any point during the game.

5. You may not pick up the football in the middle of play, unless you shoot it off the table and get a down.

6. Field goal procedure: When you get four downs or when your opponent has a chance at an extra point after a touchdown, you put your fingers in goal position. (See Illustration 10.)

10.

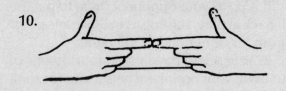

Your opponent sets the football on end (as in starting position, Illustration 7), approximately 3 inches (7.5 cm.) From the edge of table, and tries to finger-kick it between the goal posts. To avoid arguments, you are the one to decide whether the kick is good or not. A field goal is worth three extra points, unless it takes place after a touchdown, in which case it is worth only one extra point.

After a field goal, your opponent starts the ball back in play, beginning at his or her edge of the table (with the ball in position as in Illustration 7 or 8).

PENNY SOCCER

PLAYERS: 2
**EQUIPMENT: 3 or more coins. (You can play
     with all pennies or any other group of
     coins. Playing with a variety of coins in
     the same game is more interesting.)
     A table
     Pen or pencil**

You, sitting at one end of the table, are the Defender. You place your index finger and pinky on the edge of the table, with your middle fingers bent underneath (like this):

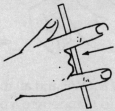

The space between your fingers on the table is the Goal.

Your opponent—the Attacker—sits at the other end of the table, and arranges the pennies in either this order:

    or this order:

THE FIRST MOVE: The Attacker—with four fingers bent—pushes or flip-pushes the pennies, just enough to break the formation and prepare for the next move.

THE SECOND MOVE and all the moves after that: are used to manoeuvre a penny into the Defender's goal. The Attacker may use any finger or fingers to shoot the penny through, but not his or her thumb. The Attacker gets as many turns as it takes (no one counts them), as long as the Attacker doesn't break any of the rules.

THE RULES

1. The penny that the Attacker shoots must go in a path between the other two pennies.

2. The penny must not touch either of the other two pennies.

3. If the Attacker has a difficult shot to make—a curve, for example—the player may use a pen or pencil to assist the shot. In the illustration below you see the problem the Attacker is up against.

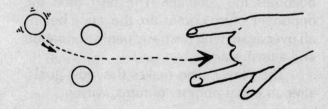

Here you see how you can use a pen to solve it.

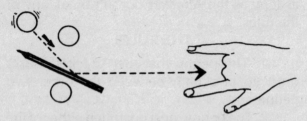

4. The penny may not go off the table.

5. To be a goal, the penny must hit the backboard (your knuckles).

The players take turns trying to shoot a goal. If the Attacker breaks one of the rules, his or her turn is over and the Defender becomes the Attacker. The next time the opponent's turn comes up, the game begins all over again with the basic penny formation and a fresh start.

The player who makes the most goals, after an equal number of turns, wins.

HAND WRESTLE

PLAYERS: 2 or more
EQUIPMENT: None

You can hand wrestle anywhere. First, two players stand opposite each other, each with right foot forward and legs apart. They stand in the same position as for fencing.

Then the players grasp each other's right hand. (Left-handers can wrestle only against other left-handers.) While holding right hands firmly, both players count to three. At the number "three," both start to turn, shove, twist and pull with their wrists, trying to throw each other off balance. The first player to move his or her right foot (that's the forward foot) loses.

If you have a large group, several hand wrestling contests can go on at the same time.

TABLE WRESTLE

PLAYERS: 2 or more
EQUIPMENT: 2 chairs for each 2 contestants
1 table for each 2 contestants

This is another strength contest.
The players sit down facing each other
on two chairs with a small sturdy table in

between. The table should be small enough so that when the players sit and reach across, they can easily touch each other's shoulders.

The players place their right elbows squarely on the table with their forearms and wrists straight up. They clasp hands. At a signal, they try to press the other's wrist down until it touches the table.

As soon as one player forces the other's wrist to the table, the contest is over. Left hands can be used only to grasp the chairs they sit on, not the table.

Left-handers should be matched up with other left-handers.

GOING UP THE WALL

PLAYERS: 2
EQUIPMENT: None

Players will need to practice this exercise often before they can master it.

First they sit on the floor with head, shoulders, and back against the wall. Then they bend their legs, and put their knees up against their chests. If possible, set up the opponents so that they are sitting against opposite walls. This way they can watch each other without getting in each other's way.

Then without using their hands to support their bodies, they work themselves up along the wall so they finish by standing with their backs against the wall. At a signal they begin, and the one who rises to a standing position first wins.

BACK TO BACK

PLAYERS: 2 or more
EQUIPMENT: None

Back to Back can be played indoors or out. It takes skill and lots of practice. Rubber-soled shoes or sneakers help players get a good grip on the ground.

Two players sit back to back with their arms folded over their chests. Then at a signal, each player tries to stand up while still keeping arms folded. The first player to do this wins.

The trick to winning is to push up against the back of the other player. The one who does this first has the advantage. Sometimes a player with a better sense of balance can win over a stronger player.

Several pairs of players in a group can try this stunt at the same time. Then the winners

can be matched with each other and a final
winner chosen.

OVER THE LINE

PLAYERS: 2 or more
EQUIPMENT: Tape

Two players at a time (or two teams) can test their strength in this pulling contest. You can play it in a gym or outdoors.

Mark on the floor with tape two parallel goal lines 20 feet (6m) apart. Two players start by facing each other exactly midway between the two goal lines. At a signal, each player grabs the other's wrists and tries to pull the player back across his or her own goal line. The first player to pull the opponent over the goal line two out of three times wins.

If a player pulls his or her hand free, then both must go all the way back to the middle and start again. So hold tight when you get your opponent near your goal line.

MORE GREAT GAMES

20 QUESTIONS

PLAYERS: 2 or more
EQUIPMENT: None

Twenty Questions is a far better game than most people realize if you use a little imagination when you choose your subject. It is one of the simplest guessing games, and people of all ages can play it.

One person thinks of a creature, place, or thing and announces to the group whether it is animal, vegetable, or mineral.

Animal is anything from a human being to a sponge in the "animal kingdom," but it can also be anything made from animal skin (like a leather wallet) to part of an animal, like the great white shark's jaws or a strip of bacon. It can also be groups of people—like all the people who live in downtown Burbank, or all the people who go out on

blind dates. It can be a supernatural creature, like Superman or Frankenstein, or a nursery rhyme character like Mary, Mary, Quite Contrary. It can also be part of a fictional person, like Dracula's tooth.

Vegetable is anything in the plant

kingdom. It can be something that grows on trees or in the ground. It can be something made from things that grow—like paper or a book, or perfume, or spaghetti. It can also be penicillin (made from bread mold), a hot water bottle, or skis—or some specific thing, like the Pines of Rome, the poison apple the Wicked Queen prepared for Snow White, or all the French fries that McDonald's serves in a year.

Mineral is just about everything else— rocks and stones, but also water, salt, glass, plastic, or the Emerald City of Oz.

Back to the game: One player announces the classification of the subject and then the guessers get 20 questions in which to find out what it is. The questions must be ones that can be answered "Yes," "No," "Partly," or "Sometimes." The player who guesses what it is becomes the next player to select the subject.

BOTTICELLI

PLAYERS: 2 to 10
EQUIPMENT: None

Botticelli (pronounced Bah-ti-CHELL-ee) is
one of the great guessing games, and can be
played by anyone from age 8 up. The more
knowledgeable the group, the more fun.

One player thinks of a person, real or
fictional, living or dead, and tells the group
only the first letter of the person's last name.
The others have to guess who it is, but they
are only allowed to guess if they already have
someone in mind. For instance, let's say the
subject is Botticelli, the Italian artist. Here is
part of a game:

MARK: I am a famous person whose name begins with B.

HAL: Are you a famous composer?

(He is thinking of Beethoven.)

MARK: No, I am not Bach.

LIZ: Are you a character from the comics?

MARK: No, I am not Charlie Brown.

LAEL: Are you a comedy writer?

MARK: No, I am not Mel Brooks.

JIM: Are you an actor?

MARK: No, I am not Charles Bronson.

HAL: *(Still trying for Beethoven but he can't ask the same question the same way twice).* Are you a composer who went deaf?

MARK: No, I am not Beethoven.

(Hal revealed too much. It would have been better if he had known some obscure fact about Beethoven that would disguise his idea so that Mark would not have thought of Beethoven so easily.)

LIZ: Are you a U.S. President?

MARK: *(stumped)* I challenge you.

LIZ: Buchanan!

(Liz, having stumped Mark, gets a leading question, which will help the group find out who Mark is. The leading question must be one that can be answered "yes" or "no.")

LIZ: Are you male?

MARK: Yes.

(Must answer a leading question truthfully.)

LAEL: Are you a famous painter?

(She is thinking of Botticelli.)

MARK: Yes, but I am not Bosch.

(Mark had to admit that Lael had guessed the right category. But he didn't have to admit that he was Botticelli as long as he could think of another painter beginning with B.)

JIM: Are you a famous general?

MARK: *(stumped again)* I challenge you.

JIM: Napoleon Bonaparte! I get a leading question. Are you alive?

MARK: No.

Well, you get the idea . . .

ANAGRAMS

PLAYERS: 2 to 4
EQUIPMENT: A set of Anagrams, which usually
can be purchased inexpensively, or you
can make your own from cardboard. Each
cutout should be about an inch square and
you can print a letter on one side. (See
note below.)
PREPARATION: Set all the anagram squares face
down on the table.

Each person picks up one letter to see who
goes first. The one with the lowest letter (A is
the best) gets to turn over the letters one by
one and set them out on a table so that
everyone sees them at the same time. Player
#1—Ken—keeps turning up letters until he or
another of the players—Verlyn—sees the
possibility of making a word of four or more
letters. The first player to call out a word—
let's say it is Verlyn—gets the word for her

own. She places it in her corner of the table.

Verlyn is now the one to turn up the letters, and she continues until another word is seen by one of the players, in which case that player takes the word and gets to turn over the letters.

Players may steal words at any time by adding a letter from the table to any existing words. For example, suppose Ken has the word POOL and an "S" shows up on the table. Verlyn has been waiting for an "S," hoping to steal that word. She says quickly, "Stealing POOL," and makes the word SPOOL, which she puts in her column of words. She couldn't steal POOL with POOLS, because a "steal" really has to change the meaning of a word, not just lengthen it. When she steals, however, she doesn't get a chance to turn up letters; all she gets is the word itself.

Players should keep all their words in

full view at all times so that other players can steal them.

If your Anagram set has number values on the letters, count your score by totalling up those number values. This makes the game much more interesting. Each vowel, for example, is worth only one point, because there are so many of them in the game. The more often-used consonants—N, R, S, and T—are worth only 1 point, too. Worth 2 points each are D, G, H, and L; for B, C, F, M, and P you get 3; for Y you get 4; for J, K and V, you get 8; for Q, X and Z—10.

Highest score wins.

Note: If you can't find an Anagram set and need to make your own, you may want to follow this guide in making up the letters: A–13, B–4, C–4, D–8, E–20, F–4, G–6, H–5, I–13, J–2, K–2, L–6, M–4, N–10, O–13, P–3, Q–2, R–10, S–6, T–9, U–8, V–2, X–1, Y–3, Z–2.

MANCALA

PLAYERS: 2
**EQUIPMENT: 14 cupcake holders—or jar tops—
    or any other small container-like holder
    18 pennies or marbles**

Mancala originated in ancient Egypt and is one of the oldest games in the world. You can play it on a special Mancala board, if you have one, or by using any small contain- ers you have at hand. (Or if you're outdoors, by scooping out little holes in the earth.)

Set out your "board" like this:

Put 3 pennies in each "hole" except for the end ones. These end holes are common property, and belong to both players.

One player—Scott—starts, scooping up all the pennies from one of the holes on his side of the board and distributing them—one penny to a hole—in each hole to the right, including the holes on the end.

The winner is the first player to get rid of all the pennies on his or her side of the board.

If Scott's last penny falls into the end hole, he goes again. He can choose any hole on his side of the board, scoop out the pennies, and distribute them one by one in the holes to the right.

If his penny lands in a hole which is on the other player's side of the board, and there is no penny at all in that hole, Scott gets to scoop out the opposite hole (on his side of the board) and distribute the pennies in it. If he has no pennies there, his turn is over.

ESP

PLAYERS: 2
EQUIPMENT: A book with full-page illustrations
    or a magazine

Maybe you do have ESP!

Choose a quiet time and a quiet mood and put your psychic powers to a test that may—as the ads say—amaze you with its results. One of you should select a book with illustrations in it, preferably full-page illustrations, but don't say what book it is that you have chosen. You could use a magazine, too, with full-page ads.

Open the book to an illustration and ask your partner a specific question concerning it, such as, "How many people (or animals or houses) are in the picture I'm looking at?"

Now concentrate as hard as you can on the number of people in the picture while your partner concentrates on trying to read your mind. The answer may be right or wrong, but in either case, go on to the next question. Don't make a guessing game of it. If the answer is wrong, just say "No, there are two people. I am now going to concentrate on what one of them is doing. Try to tell me what that is."

The results may truly astound you, especially if the first answer should happen to be correct. That will give you both a feeling of self-confidence that adds a tremendous impetus to your psychic powers. If you don't seem to get anywhere, change roles and let your partner choose another book and "send" a picture to you by thought transference.

ALL ABOUT YOU!

By the way you answer the questions in the following "tests," supposedly the psychologist will be able to tell you all about yourself. The tests are silly, and have nothing to do with real psychology, but they are fun at parties and get people laughing and talking.

Ask all the questions before you tell people what they "reveal."

WALKING IN THE WOODS

You are walking through the woods when you come to a clearing. In the clearing, there is a lake, and beside the lake, there is a cup. You are thirsty.

1. What do you do:
    a. Use the cup to take a drink from the lake?
    b. Leave the cup where it is?
    c. Examine the cup in order to decide what to do?

2. Then do you—
    a. Put the cup back where it was?
    b. Leave it where it is?
    c. Take the cup away with you?

The water in the lake looks inviting. You are warm.

3. Do you—
    a. Wash your face and hands in it?
    b. Go swimming in it?
    c. Stay out of it?

You see a bear approaching as you stand by the lake. He is walking slowly and evidently doesn't see you.

4. Do you—
    a. Run as fast as you can?
    b. Stand very still?
    c. Try to make friends with the bear?

Analyses on pages 342–343

IN A DREAM GARDEN

1. Describe your dream garden.
2. Where is your house in relation to the garden?
3. What is the house like?
4. What is the key to your house like?
5. What would you do if you lost your key and wanted to get into your house?
6. You are standing alone holding something. What is it?
7. Near your garden is a house that belongs to someone else. It has a wall around it. There is a gate in the wall and a lock on the gate and you have no key for this lock. You want to get in. What would you do?

Analyses on pages 343–344

READING TEA LEAVES

**EQUIPMENT: A cup of tea which has been
brewed from real tea (not a tea bag)**

You have to use your imagination when
you read tea leaves! If you see a pattern that
reminds you of a mask, for example, you
might announce that the person is going to
get a part in a play, or be invited to a costume
party (especially if you know one is coming
up). You could get very psychological and
say the person is hiding his or her real self. If
you see a door, you could say there will be a
change—old doors closing and new ones
opening up. If the specks remind you of a
kangaroo, you might advise looking before
leaping—or moving rapidly (in leaps and

bounds) to a goal. Don't be afraid to make up vague nonsense. It may sound silly to you, but your friends will take it very seriously. Because of that , you need to be careful not to go around scaring people. Keep your predictions happy ones.

Here are a few symbols that you can keep in mind for the times when you really don't see much in the cup:

Anchor: Good results from your plan.

Clover Leaf: Good luck. If it is at the top of the cup as you look at it, it is coming soon. If it is at the bottom, there will be a delay.

Clouds: If they are thick, delay. If they are light, good results.

Cross: If it is at the top of the cup, without clouds around it, good luck is coming soon. If at the bottom, troubles over which you will triumph.

Dog: At the top, faithful friends. If surrounded with clouds and dashes, a false friend. At the bottom: Be careful not to make anyone jealous or you'll be sorry.

Flower: If at the top or in the middle of the cup, you have or will have a good marriage. If it is at the bottom, anger.

Letter: In the clear, you'll have good news soon. With dots around it, money is coming. Hemmed in by clouds, bad news.

Moon: If it is clear, high honors; if it is clouded over, disappointment that will pass. If at the bottom of the cup, good fortune.

Mountains: One mountain signifies powerful friends. More than one—powerful enemies. If they are clear, friends who have authority.

Snake: At the top or in the middle: If you act honorably, your enemies will not triumph over you. If surrounded by clouds, watch your temper and your actions carefully to avoid trouble.

Star: Happiness. With dots around it: Good fortune.

Sun: Luck and happiness. Surrounded by dots, a great change in your life.

Tree: Good health. A group of trees wide apart: You will get your wish. With dashes around them: Your good luck has already begun. With dots: Riches.

FORTUNE-TELLING WITH DOMINOES

This ancient method of telling fortunes is limited. You can only do it once a month, and never on Friday or Monday. When you can do it, you may only draw 3 dominoes at a sitting. Break the rules and the answers will be wrong.

Shuffle the dominoes around the table—facedown—before selecting one. Before you select a second domino, shuffle them around again.

If you select

6-6: You will marry someone rich and have many children.

6-5: Don't be discouraged. Even if the person you love rejects you, you will eventually succeed.

6-4: Early marriage and much happiness.

6-3: Love. Happiness. Riches. Honors.

6-2: Happy marriage. Luck in business. Bad luck for thieves.

6-1: Two marriages. The second one will be happier.

6-: Blank: Loss of a friend.

5-5: Luck. Success, but not necessarily money.

5-4: Not good for money matters. You will marry someone poor or someone who has expensive tastes.

5-3: Comfortable marriage. You will never be poor.

5-2: Misfortune in love. If you marry the one you love, it may not work out.

5-1: You will receive an invitation and you will enjoy yourself very much. Not good for money matters.

5-: Blank: For a female: sorrow through the affections. For a male: difficult financial conditions.

4-4: An invitation (to a party?) at which you will have a wonderful time.

4-3: You will marry young and live happily.

4-2: A big change in your life. If you quarreled with a friend, you will make up and be better friends than before.

4-1: Happy marriage.

4-: Blank: Bad for love affairs. This foretells quarrels and separations. Don't tell your secret; it won't be kept.

3-3: Riches.

3-2: Good for love and travel.

3-1: Secret love affairs.

3-: Blank: Invitation (to a party?) at which you will meet someone new. If you marry, difficult mate.

2-2: Success in love. Happiness in marriage. Success, but not necessarily money.

2-1: For a female: You will marry young and live a life of luxury. For a male: Lucky in love.

2-: Blank: Bad luck. For females: Good luck if you live alone. Safe voyage. Possible accident, but protection against physical injury.

1-1: Affection and happiness in love and marriage.

1-: Blank: Sorrow in love. Disappointment.

HOW TO TELL FORTUNES WITH DICE

EQUIPMENT: 3 dice
   A dice cup or box
   A board
   A piece of chalk
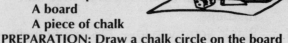
PREPARATION: Draw a chalk circle on the board

This method of telling fortunes is less restricted than the domino method on page 312, but it also has its limitations. You may not use it on days that are unlucky for dice—Mondays and Wednesdays.

Put the dice in the dice cup and shake it with your left hand. Then throw the dice into the chalk circle. You read the message by counting the number of spots on the top of the three dice and checking the total in the following list.

If you get the same number twice, you will get news from someone far away.

If you throw the dice out of the chalk circle, don't bother to count the totals. It means you will have a quarrel.

If the dice fall on the floor, it will be a violent quarrel.

If one die lands on top of the other, the answer is negative.

If you throw:

3: Success in love. Many lovers.

4: Many lovers, but you will not be perfectly pleased with any of them.

5: Obstacles or quarrels in love.

6: Many lovers, exciting life.

7: Luck in money matters.

8: Stinginess. Whoever throws it will never be poor, but may live poorly through miserliness.

9: Good luck in everything—except games of chance.

10: Good luck. If a young girl throws it, she will not marry soon. She will have good luck in other matters. If a married woman

throws it, she may get a legacy. If a man
throws it, good luck in love.

11: Extravagance. Waste of money.

12: An event of some kind, happy or unhappy.
Has nothing to do with matters of love.

13: Be suspicious. People around you may not
be trustworthy.

14: If a female throws it: Unhappy marriage.
Good life if she stays single.
For a man: Dishonesty, lack of principles.

15: Bad luck in speculation. Good luck in
marriage.

16: Bad luck in business. Good luck in
marriage.

17: You won't find the property you lost. Good
luck in your work. Disappointment,
otherwise.

18: Riches, honors, a happy life. Good luck in
love and in your work. Bad luck for
thieves.

OPTICAL ILLUSIONS

Changing Images
It depends upon whether you place your attention on the dark or light color. Either one can be the background.

Three Movie Buffs
They are all the same height. The man at the right looks tallest. We expect things to look smaller when they are farther away. The man at the right is farthest away and we would expect him to look the smallest. Since he doesn't, we assume he's really larger.

Sick Circle
Nothing. It is an exact circle, but when it is broken by other lines, our eyes are distracted and follow the new lines instead of the original circle.

Bulging Square
No. Our eyes cannot separate the figure from the intercepting arcs. Nevertheless, it is a perfect square.

The Fence
Inside the black squares, you see an even blacker lattice design! Why?

After you concentrate on a picture for a while, your eyes get tired. The most tired parts are certain spots on the "retina," the part of the eye which contains light-sensitive cells. The brightest tones cause the greatest stress to these cells, which gradually become less sensitive to light. When you look away from the white lines, the nerve-ends that are less tired lightly reproduce the darker sections of the picture. Your eye transforms a negative into a positive. Here you have become tired of seeing the white lines. Your eyes record the black instead, when you shift your attention.

Warped Bars
They are perfectly straight.

What's on White?
Grey dots appear at the point where white meets white. The white lines look bright when they contrast with the black areas. When white meets white, therefore, they are less bright, and the grey dots show up.

Nightmare Forest
They are straight. Tilt the book all the way back and you'll have proof!

Mad Hat

They are the same. Usually we overestimate vertical distance, whether it's the distance from a house roof to a plane or just the drawing on the page.

Cut-Outs

"A" seems larger, but they are both the same size. Our tendency is to compare the base of "B" with the top arch of "A".

Unsure Lines

1. Yes, but when you break a straight line with a solid bar, the straight line seems displaced.
2. "B" is the continuation of "A." "C" looks as though it connects with "A" because the solid bar "displaces" the line.

The Staircase

Depending on how you focus on the letters, the staircase can run up from A to B or you could be standing beneath the upside-down version. To see it upside down, focus on the A.

Looking Around

Either one.

Four Detectives

The four detectives have equally large mouths.

Hidden Shapes

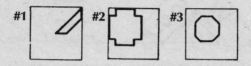

The Spoke-Wheel Phenomenon

As you turn or as your eyes tire, the overlapping images cause you to see "moiré" (plane propeller) designs within the circles.

Big Wheels

The circles spin to the right. Many people say the cogwheel turns to the left; others say it stands still.

Count the Cubes

Both. There are 8 cubes with black tops or 7 cubes with white bottoms. It depends on how you look at it.

#5

```
M A R S . A T A . C H A T
O H I O . R E N . L I S A
P A D S . C A T W O M A N
. . D O I T . S E W . . .
P A L . N I P . I N P U T
O L E . S C O U R . E S E
P A R K A . E N D . N A N
. . . A N D . L O N G . .
M R F R E E Z E . A U N T
R O L E . N O S . B I B S
S W A N . S O S . S N A P
```

#6

```
S A G S . E S P . . A S A
E X I T . R A I L . G A G
W E R E . A N T E L O P E
. . A P E S . T O E . . .
O F F . T E N . E G G S .
A L F . C R U S T . O A K
R Y E S . T E A . R B I .
. . . I A M . A N D I . .
E L E P H A N T . A L S O
N E W . S M E E . S L A W
D I E . A D D . H A T E .
```

#7

```
S C A B . M O P S . T I M
H O L E . A L I E . A W E
A B L E . S I T E . B I D
F R E N C H V A N I L L A
T A N . B E E . C E L L .
. . . E S S . J O E . . .
S I F T . T O N . C D S .
C H O C O L A T E C H I P
R A Y . W E S T . L I M E
A T E . L A T E . A M E N
P E R . S P E D . P E S T
```

#8

```
O F F . H I P . . S T A Y
M E L . A C E S . O H I O
A L I . T E N T . N E R D
H O N K S . N O T . S E A
A N T I . P Y R A M I D .
. . S T A R . E X A M . .
. S T E R E O S . S P A S
W H O . T A R . I S S U E
R A N T . C E N T . O D E
E V E N . H O E S . N I P
N E S T . S T Y . S O S .
```

#9

```
L O C K S . I T S . B U Y
A N N I E . A R E . A S A
S A N T A . M O M . S A M
. . . E T C . M I S S . .
A C T . S L A B . O O P S
S O R T . A G O . B O R E
H O U R . R E N T . N O T
. . . M I N I . E A R . .
Z I P . A N D . M O R A L
A C E . P E A . E L O P E
G E T . S T Y . S E W E D
```

The Man in the Elevator

The man is a dwarf. He can reach the button in the elevator for the first floor, but he cannot reach the button for the tenth floor. The seventh-floor button is the highest he can reach.

Bombs Away!

The bomber was flying upside down.

The Coal, Carrot, and Scarf

They were used by children who made a snowman. The snow has now melted.

Death in the Phone Booth

He was describing to a friend the size of a fish that got away. In his enthusiasm, he put his hands through the windows, thereby accidentally slitting his wrists.

The Silent Cabbie

He must have heard her initial instructions or he would not have known where to take her.

The Men in the Hotel
Mr. Jones could not sleep because Mr. Smith was snoring. His phone call awoke Mr. Smith and stopped him snoring long enough for Mr. Jones to get to sleep.

A Peculiar House
The builder built the house at the North Pole!

The Man in the House
The man was a burglar intent on robbing the house. When he reached the library, he heard a harsh voice say, "Hands up!" When he looked around, he saw a parrot in a cage.

A Chess Piece
Who said that they were playing each other?

The Unseen Walker
He walked through the sewers.

The Two Sisters
When they had finished the cleaning, they had no mirror to look at, so each girl looked at her sister. The girl with the clean face saw that her sister was dirty and assumed that she would be dirty, so she washed. Her sister made the reverse assumption.

The Dream

The sacked employee was the warehouse night watchman. He should have been awake all night on his security duties. Having a dream proved that he was asleep on the job. For this, he was fired.

In the Pet Shop

There was a price list on the wall. It showed poodle puppies at eight dollars, Labradors at nine dollars, and Alsatians at 10 dollars. The first man put a ten-dollar bill on the counter, so he could have wanted any of the three breeds. The second man put down one five-dollar bill and five one-dollar bills. The assistant correctly deduced that the second man wanted the Alsatian.

The Coffee Drinker

He had sweetened the original cup of coffee with sugar. He therefore knew when he tasted the coffee that it was the same cup.

Happy or Sad

It was the finals of the Miss World Beauty Contest. The winner always cries. The disappointed runners-up smile because everyone is watching them and they are expected to look happy and radiant.

One Step Beyond
He started off outside the window and leapt into the building. Why was he outside? He could either have been on the ledge contemplating suicide or he could have been the window cleaner. Take your pick.

The Turkish Bath Mystery
John was murdered by Jack, who brought an ice dagger into the Turkish Baths in his thermos flask. The dagger melted away after the murder, leaving no clue.

The Single Statement
The explorer made the statement, "I will be eaten by lions." Now, if the chief does feed him to the lions, his statement will have been true, so he should be thrown off the cliff. But if he is thrown off the cliff, his statement will have been false. The chief had to admit that the only fair course of action was to let the explorer go free.

Death in Rome
Mr. Jones was a travel agent. He had recently supplied by post two plane tickets for Mr. Rigby-Brown. The two tickets were for Rome, but the one for Mr. Rigby-Brown had been ordered as a return ticket. Mrs. Rigby-Brown's ticket had been one way only.

WORD SEARCH PUZZLES

The Simpsons

330

Circling the Bases

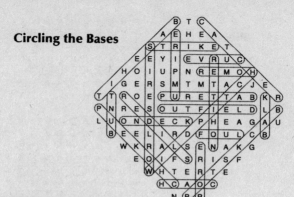

Monopoly Game

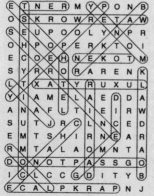

331

Piece a Pizza

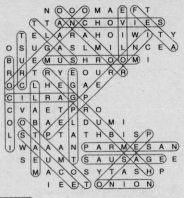

By the Numbers

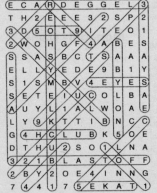

332

Modern Electronics

Feeling Lucky?

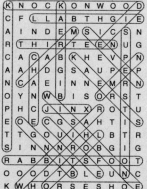

333

"Oh, Horrors!"

Famous Last Words

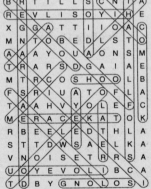

334

BAKER STREET PUZZLES

Happy Birthday, Dear Sherlock
> December 31.

Wishing Well
> 28 hours.

Order of Finish
> 1st   Royal Mile
> 2nd Manor Park
> 3rd Peanuts
> 4th Dusky
> and finally,
>   Eastern Classic

Three Thieves
> Ealing and the silver coins.

Message from Moriarty
> Each letter in the code represents the letter
> that it follows in the alphabet. Therefore, the
> code reads: "I will rob the Bank of England
> tonight. Moriarty."

Snooker

Holmes with 29 points, followed by Watson with 22 points, Lestrade with 21 points, and the sergeant with 18 points.

Country Dinner

The actress was Handy.

The Safety Deposit Box

Number 22

20 (x4) = 80 (-4) = 76 (:4) = 19 (+4) = 23 (x4) = 92 (-4) = 88 (:4) = 22.

Victim Meeting

1. Brown/Banker
2. Adams/Solicitor
3. Clark/Doctor
4. Dawson/Vet
5. Smith/Baker
6. Jones/Dentist
7. Black/Butcher
8. Wilson/Surgeon

More from Moriarty

Number 264 Baker Street.

Synchronize Your Watches!

20 hours.

Who's Who at the Table?

Georgina.

Library Books

Holmes: GREAT CRIMINALS
Watson: GREAT DETECTIVES
Hudson: MEDICINE
Moriarty: POLICE
Lestrade: THE COOK BOOK

The Case of the Hard-boiled Egg

Drop the egg into boiling water. At the same time, start the 7-minute hourglass and the 11-minute hourglass. When the 7-minute hour glass runs out, turn it over. When the 11-minute hourglass runs out, turn the 7-minute hourglass again. When the 7-minute hourglass runs out, 15 minutes will have passed.

WORD HUNT

AMELIORATE

alarm	item	mart	more	rialto	tiara
alate	lair	martial	mortal	riata	tile
alit	lama	mate	mote	rile	time
altar	lame	mater	motel	rime	timer
alto	lariat	material	omelet	riot	tire
aorta	late	meal	omit	rite	toil
area	later	meat	oral	roam	toile
aerate	leer	mere	orate	roil	tole
areole	liar	merit	rail	role	tome
aria	lime	metal	rate	rote	tore
aril	lira	meteor	ratel	tail	trail
aroma	liter	meter	ratio	tailor	trailer
atelier	loam	mile	real	tale	tram
earl	loiter	mire	realm	tame	tremor
elate	lore	mite	ream	tare	trial
elite	mail	mitre	reel	taro	trim
emir	male	moat	relate	teal	trio
emit	mare	mole	remit	team	
emote	marital	moral	teem	tear	
irate	marl	morale	retail	term	

IRREGULARLY

ague	gall	grill	layer	rare	rill
airy	gallery	gruel	leary	rarely	rule
alley	gayer	guile	legal	real	ruler
ally	gear	gull	liar	really	ruly
argue	girl	gully	lira	rear	rural
argyle	glare	gyre	lure	regal	ugly
aril	glue	lager	lyre	regular	urge
earl	grail	lair	rage	relay	year
early	gray	large	rail	rely	yell
gale	grey	largely	rally	rile	yule

PRECIOUS

cope	cruise	pier	recoup	sire	suer
copse	cure	pious	rice	sirup	super
core	curse	pore	rise	sore	sure
corpse	cusp	poser	rope	soup	user
coup	ecru	pour	rose	sour	
coupe	epic	price	ruse	spice	
course	icer	prose	scope	spire	
crisp	osier	puce	score	spore	
crop	ours	pure	scour	spruce	
croupe	peri	purse	scrip	spur	

DEVELOPING

deep	dole	gave	liege	novel	plod
deign	dope	glen	lien	ogee	pole
deal	dove	glide	ling	ogle	pond
delve	dung	glove	lion	olden	pone
depone	edge	golden	live	olive	veil
devein	elide	gone	liven	open	vein
develop	elope	idle	lode	opine	vend
devil	endive	idol	loge	oven	vile
dine	envelop	ingle	loin	ovine	vine
ding	envied	ledge	long	pend	viol
dinge	even	legend	lope	pied	void
dive	evil	lend	love	pile	
doge	geode	levied	need	pine	
doing	gild	lied	node	plied	

CONSTRUCTION

coin	coon	croon	into	onus	rust
conic	coot	crouton	iron	oust	rustic
consort	corn	crust	noon	roost	scion
constrict	cost	curio	notion	root	scoot
construct	cotton	curt	noun	rout	scorn
contort	count	icon	occur	ruction	scour
contour	court	incur	onion	ruin	scout
confusion	cousin	instruct	onto	runt	snort

snout	stoic	suction	torso	tunic	unto
soon	stout	suit	tort	turn	
soot	strict	tint	tour	unction	
sour	strut	tocsin	tout	unicorn	
sort	stun	tonic	trot	union	
stint	stunt	toot	trout	unison	
stir	succor	torn	trust	unit	

ESTABLISH

abet	bath	east	lash	sash	stale
able	bathe	habit	lass	sate	stash
aisle	beast	hail	last	seal	steal
alit	beat	hale	late	seat	sties
asset	belt	hassle	lath	shale	stile
bail	best	hast	lathe	shall	table
bate	bias	haste	leash	shies	tail
bale	bile	hate	least	silt	tale
bait	bite	heal	less	sisal	tassel
bash	blasé	heat	lest	slab	teal
basil	blast	heist	list	slash	this
basis	bleat	hilt	sable	slat	tile
bass	bless	hiss	sahib	slate	
basset	blest	isle	sail	slit	
bast	bliss	isle	sale	slab	
baste	blithe	istle	salt	stable	

341

WALKING IN THE WOODS

Question #1 reveals your attitude towards other people. If you answered:

    (a) you are outgoing, friendly, and not always as cautious as you might be.

    (b) you wait for other people to approach you, offering your friendship only to a few.

    (c) your attitude towards others is based on common sense.

Question #2 reveals your attitude towards your friends. If you answered:

    (a) your friendships are often casual, and even when you are very friendly, you make few demands on relationships.

    (b) you are easily offended and don't open up often, even to your closest friends.

    (c) you are possessive of your friends, demanding and quite jealous.

Question #3 reveals your attitude towards experiences. If you answered:

    (a) you test out new activities before you commit yourself to them.

(b) you rush into new things and often drop them.
   (c) you are reluctant to participate in new activities and hold yourself aloof from things that might really interest you if you gave them a chance.

Question #4 reveals your attitude towards life. If you answered:
   (a) you run away from it.
   (b) you wait to see what is going to happen before taking action.
   (c) you go out to meet it, often without thinking!

IN A DREAM GARDEN

1. Your description of your ideal garden is a description of the way you want everyone to think of you.
2/3. Your description of the house and where it is in relation to the garden is a description of the way you see yourself in relation to the rest of the world.

4. Your description of the key is a description of your friendships—how simple or complicated they are.

5. What you do when you lose your key tells what you do when something goes wrong in a friendship.

6. Whatever you choose to describe represents the artistic side of your nature, your imagination.

7. The action you take reveals what you do when you are faced with an obstacle.

Index & Guide

Title	Page	Players	Type
20 Questions	290	2+	game
Accordion	104	1	solitaire game
All About You!	303	1+	game
Anagrams	296	2–4	game
Authors	146	2–5	card game
Back to Back	286	2+	game
Big Wheels	27	1	optical illusion
Bombs Away!	164	1+	mystery
Botticelli	293	2–10	game
Broken Finger	250	1+	challenge
Bulging Square	11	1	optical illusion
By the Numbers	204	1	puzzle
Calamity Jane	159	3–7	card game
Canfield	123	1	solitaire game
Case of the Hard-boiled Egg	240	1+	mystery
Cave Man Game	101	1	solitaire game
Changing Images	8	1	optical illusion
Chess Piece	169	1+	mystery
Circling the Bases	198	1	puzzle
Clock	107	1	solitaire game

Title	Page	Players	Type
Coal, Carrot, & Scarf	165	1+	mystery
Coffee Drinker	174	1+	mystery
Concentration	142	2+	card game
Count the Cubes	28	1	optical illusion
Country Dinner	226	1+	mystery
Crazy Eights	147	2–5	card game
Crosswords	57–75	1	puzzles
Cut-Outs	18	1	optical illusion
Death in Rome	179	1+	mystery
Death in the Phone Booth	165	1+	mystery
Dictionary	269	1+	game
Do As I Do	86	2	card trick
Dots	262	2	game
Double Deal	96	2+	card trick
Dream	172	1+	mystery
ESP	301	2	game
Eternal Triangles	263	1+	game
Famous Last Words	212	1	puzzle
Feeling Lucky?	208	1	puzzle
Fence	12	1	optical illusion
Fortune-Telling with Dominoes	312	1+	game

Title	Page	Players	Type
Four Detectives	22	1	optical illusion
Four-Heap Deal	91	2	card trick
Four-Leaf Clover	100	1	solitaire game
Gaps	114	1	solitaire game
Go Boom	152	2–5	
Go Fish	145	2–5	card game
Going Up the Wall	284	2	game
Hand Wrestle	281	2+	challenge
Happy Birthday, Dear Sherlock	215	1+	mystery
Happy or Sad	175	1+	mystery
Hearts	157	2–6	card game
Hidden Shapes	23	1	optical illusion
Hit Cards	103	1	solitaire game
How Old Are You?	44	2+	mind reading
How to Tell Fortunes with Dice	316	1+	game
I've Got Your Number	39	2+	mind reading
In a Dream Garden	306	1+	game
In the Pet Shop	173	1+	mystery
Irresistible Force	249	1+	challenge
Keep from Laughing	254	6+	challenge

Title	Page	Players	Type
Klondike	120	1	solitaire game
Library Books	238	1+	mystery
Lift a Friend	252	5+	challenge
Longest Word	261	2+	word game
Looking Around	21	1	optical illusion
Lucky Penny	242	1+	challenge
Mad Hat	17	1	optical illusion
Magic Number	59	2+	mind reading
Man in the Elevator	162	1+	mystery
Man in the House	169	1+	mystery
Mancala	289	2	game
Math Magic	48	2+	mind reading
Men in the Hotel	167	1+	mystery
Message from Moriarty	222	1+	mystery
Modern Electronics	208	1	puzzle
Monopoly Game	200	1	puzzle
More from Morirty	232	1+	mystery
Multiplying Cards	94	3+	card trick
Mutus Dedit Nomen Cocis	82	2	card trick
Mysterious Temple	30	3+	mind reading
Nightmare Forest	16	1	optical illusion
Nine Slips	36	3+	mind reading

Title	Page	Players	Type
Number Wizard	52	2+	mind reading
"Oh, Horrors!"	210	1	puzzle
One Step Beyond	176	1+	mystery
Order of Finish	218	1+	mystery
Over the Line	288	2+	game
Pat & Rub	244	1+	challenge
Peculiar House	168	1+	mystery
Penny Soccer	277	2	game
Perpetual Motion	116	1	solitaire game
Persian Card Game	132	2	card game
Piece a Pizza	202	1	puzzle
Pishe Pasha	138	2	card game
Pounce!	139	2–8	card game
Pyramid	109	1	solitaire game
Reading Tea Leaves	307	1+	game
Revenge	136	2	card game
Rubber Thumb	247	1+	challenge
Russian Solitaire	126	1	solitaire game
Safety Deposit Box	228	1+	mystery
Secret Number	46	3+	mind reading
Seeing through a Sealed Envelope	32	3+	mind reading
Sick Circle	10	1	optical illusion
Silent Cabbie	166	1+	mystery

Title	Page	Players	Type
Simpsons	196	1	puzzle
Single Statement	178	1+	mystery
Slap Jack	153	3–8	card game
Snakes	265	2–4	game
Snip-Snap-Snorum	155	3 +	card game
Snooker	224	1+	mystery
Spoke-Wheel Phenomenon	26	1	optical illusion
Sprouts	266	2	game
Staircase	20	1	optical illusion
Stuck to the Wall	246	1+	challenge
Synchronize Your Watches!	234	1+	mystery
Table Football	272	2	game
Table Wrestle	282	2+	game
Think Fast	255	3+	challenge
Three Movie Buffs	9	1	optical illusion
Three Thieves	220	1+	mystery
Three-Digit Miracle	42	1+	mind reading
Touchy Problem	243	1+	challenge
Turkish Bath Mystery	177	1+	mystery
Twin Brothers	7	1	optical illusion
Two Rows	77	2	card trick

Title	Page	Players	Type
Two Sisters	171	1+	mystery
Unseen Walker	170	1+	mystery
Unsure Lines	19	1	optical illusion
Victim Meeting	230	1+	mystery
Walking in the Woods	304	1+	game
War	134	2/3	card game
Warped Bars	14	1	optical illusion
What's on White?	15	1	optical illusion
Who's Who at the Table?	236	1+	mystery
Wild Jacks	152	2–5	card game
Wish	117	1	solitaire game
Wishing Well	216	1+	mystery
Word Hunt	258	1+	word game
Word Search Puzzles	195–212	1	puzzle